EVERYDAY JUMPING

—— FOR ——

EVERYDAY JUMPING

FOR

RIDERS AND INSTRUCTORS

MELISSA TROUP
BA, BHSII

KENILWORTH PRESS

Published in Great Britain by
Kenilworth Press, an imprint of Quiller Publishing Ltd

British Library Cataloguing in Publication Data
A catalogue record for this book is available from the British Library.

ISBN 1-872119-95-6
        978-1-872119-95-3

Layout and typesetting by Kenilworth Press
Diagrams by Michael J. Stevens
Colour drawings and cover illustration by Dianne Breeze
Photos © Melissa Troup

Printed and bound in Malta on behalf of Compass Press

KENILWORTH PRESS
An imprint of Quiller Publishing Ltd
Wykey House, Wykey, Shrewsbury, SY4 1JA
tel: 01939 261616 fax: 01939 261606
e-mail: info@quillerbooks.com
website: www.kenilworthpress.co.uk

CONTENTS

ACKNOWLEDGEMENTS

I would like to give special thanks to all those at Liege Manor Equestrian Centre who agreed to be photographed for the book. Some of the pictures are not the most flattering and yet, for the sake of the book, these generous people allowed them to be published (albeit through gritted teeth)!

Doc – many thanks. Your patient Photoshop tuition helped to produce the photos for the book.

I am also grateful to Michael Stevens and Dianne Breeze for providing such brilliant diagrams and illustrations.

AUTHOR'S NOTE

This book has been written to offer basic but comprehensive training advice for those working towards Riding Club or the lower levels of British Show Jumping Association competitions.

It is also written for the many riders who have no desire to compete, but who enjoy jumping with their horses and wish to further their ability and knowledge.

It provides numerous achievable exercises to add variety and interest to everyday jumping sessions. It also includes many exercises that are suitable for instructors to use in group or private lessons.

I strongly believe, however, that there is no substitute for jumping lessons from a qualified instructor, and suggest that this book should be used in conjunction with supervised tuition.

MELISSA TROUP
BA, BHSII

The book assumes the use of a 20m x 40m arena, but each exercise can be adapted for a differently sized school.

1 THE STAGES OF A JUMP

APPROACH – TAKE-OFF – JUMP – LANDING – DEPARTURE

In order for horse and rider to make improvements in their jumping ability, two considerations must first be analysed:

1. The demands made on the horse when jumping, and the way in which the horse copes with these demands, be they physical or mental, or both.

2. Any areas of weakness within the five stages of the jump and the way in which they affect the stages that follow.

The horse's jump

As the horse **approaches** an obstacle, he focuses on it. Without conscious assessment as we understand it, he assesses the ground line, the height and the width of the fence in order to calculate the jumping effort required.

The horse may lose focus for many different reasons:

- A sudden distraction.

- The visual effect of the fence. The fence may look 'scary' to the horse. Water trays, for example, sometimes cause problems to the horse if they are not introduced correctly.

- The horse focuses on the fence beyond the one that you are approaching, such as the second part of a double.

- The horse's head is too high on the approach, inhibiting his ability to see the fence. This often happens with a horse that rushes at the fences. The rider pulls on the reins, and as a result the horse's head comes up.

As the horse reaches the point of **take-off**, his hind legs propel him upwards and forwards. He lifts up his shoulders, helping to lift the forelegs, which he folds up underneath him. If the horse is jumping the first part of a double, at this point, and over the fence, he should be focusing on the next jump.

During the **jump**, the horse stretches his head and neck out in front of him. This allows his back to be sufficiently supple for the hind legs to fold up and follow through over the fence. If a fence worries the horse, you may find that he looks down at it as he jumps, rather than focusing ahead, and he may give it a lot of clearance.

As the horse descends, the head and neck rise slightly, for balance, and the front legs straighten and absorb the impact of **landing**. The horse's inertia moves him over his front legs, allowing the hind legs to step through and propel him forwards into the departure from the fence.

If there is a fence following shortly afterwards, such as in a related distance (see page 65), the horse should be focused on this, assessing it. During the

The approach. The horse assesses the fence.

The point of take-off. The horse's hind legs step underneath to propel him upwards and forwards.

The take-off. The horse lifts up through the shoulders and forelegs.

The jump. The horse stretches through the neck and back.

The landing. The horse's head and neck lift to aid balance.

The departure. The horse should depart in balance and rhythm. This horse is a little 'downhill'. His rider could help him by raising her upper body and keeping a supportive contact.

NOTE: This rider has longer stirrups than are suggested normally. However, her lower leg is secure and the resulting position during the jump does not inhibit the horse.

departure, the horse should immediately find the balance and rhythm in the canter, equal to that of the approach.

Summarising the stages

The **approach** sets the horse up for the next four stages of the jump. The **take-off** point is generally a reflection of the quality of the canter on the approach, and preference of the individual horse, depending on its technique over the fence. The **jump** will be a combined result of the approach, the take-off, the quality of the canter and the horse's jumping technique. The **landing** and **departure** will be the result of the approach, the take-off and the jump.

Why the approach is critical

As the five stages are intrinsically linked, the approach is critical to the success of the jump. Improvements in the quality of the canter, rider position and jumping technique are covered in later chapters in this book. This chapter aims to highlight the effect of various common problems on the approach to the fence.

A **good approach** consists of:

- A good **quality canter,** in front of the leg. This means that the horse is responsive to the aids and forward-thinking.

- A **balanced** and **rhythmical** canter through the **turn** and the **straight line** towards the fence.

- The horse being channelled between leg and hand, aiming for the **centre** of the fence.

The turn

The **turn** should place you on a **straight line** to the **centre** of the fence. Throughout the turn the horse should maintain **balance, rhythm, impulsion, straightness** and **suppleness**, and these elements should then continue into the straight line to the centre of the fence. Often one or more of these elements is lost during the turn. If one is lost, then the rest often follow suit as a result. Turns should be practised on the flat before trying to ride turns into a fence.

PROBLEM 1

The horse loses impulsion or accelerates during the turn. Both of these problems are normally due to a loss of balance through the turn.

SUGGESTIONS

- Is the turn too sharp? It is very hard for a horse to maintain his balance during a sharp turn. With the loss of balance comes the loss of rhythm and then impulsion. The horse may accelerate to try to balance himself. Try riding a larger, sweeping turn, and support at all times by keeping the horse balanced and forwards between leg and hand.

- Check that your position is not influencing the horse negatively by becoming unbalanced through the turn.

PROBLEM 2

The horse falls in/out through the shoulder during the turn.

SUGGESTIONS

- Check your own position throughout the turn.

- If the horse falls out, use the outside aids – your outside leg and hand – more effectively through the turn, so that you are thinking of bringing the horse's shoulders around. Try turning earlier and ride a softer corner.

- If the horse falls in during the turn, ride with more consideration of inside leg into outside rein to maintain balance.

The straight line into the fence

PROBLEM 3

The horse drifts to the left or right on the approach to the fence.

SUGGESTIONS

- Look at your own position. If you are leaning to one side, this will influence the horse.

- Is the rider noticeably stronger on one side of his body than the other? As the rider you should maintain the horse's straightness through an even contact on the reins and pressure with the legs.

- Does the horse drift when ridden on the threequarter or centre line during flatwork? If so, then the solution needs to be found on the flat before progressing to jumping.

- The drift may occur as a result of loss of straightness during the turn.

'Seeing a stride'

We cannot discuss the approach without considering the concept of 'seeing a stride'. 'Seeing a stride' refers to the ability to see or feel whether

the canter stride will reach the fence at a good point of take-off. This 'feel' usually occurs several strides before the fence, when the rider is able to influence the canter as necessary, either to shorten or lengthen it. If a rider sees the stride only just before the fence, there is no influence to be had over the horse, because it is too late.

Some riders are naturally gifted at seeing a stride, others are not. Some riders who can see a stride say it is more a curse than a help. If you can see that a stride is wrong, but feel incapable of doing anything about it, the horse is likely to stop, purely for the reason that you have frozen. Whereas a rider who can't see the stride is wrong, rides forward, maintaining a rhythm, and the horse either jumps from a longer take-off point, or puts in a short stride. Either way, the pair has more chance of jumping the fence through positive riding.

Jumping regularly may, in time, develop your feel for reaching the correct take-off point for the horse. Never worry if you do not have the ability to 'see a stride'. Ride the rhythm rather than actively look for a stride. In this way, the horse is taught to see the stride for himself, and will learn to adjust as necessary. Remember that horses have more natural ability to see their stride than we do. In the wild, it is essential during flight from a predator that the horse assesses an obstacle in his path and jumps it cleanly to escape.

The correct take-off point

There is a theoretically correct take-off point for each fence. However, each horse being an individual, this point may not suit all. The horse's

Good take-off and landing. The take-off point is the same distance away from the base of the fence as the landing, and the angle of ascent and descent are a mirror of each other.

technique will influence his most desired take-off point. The guidelines below will therefore need to be adjusted for each individual.

A VERTICAL

The theoretically correct take-off point for a vertical is the same distance away from the base of the fence, as the height of the fence. This theory applies

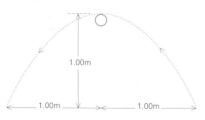

Theoretical correct take-off point for a vertical is the same distance away as the height of the fence.

to fences up to about 1.10m high. Above that the take-off distance is usually less than the fence height. For example, a horse attempting a 1.50m vertical would not take off 1.50m before the fence. High-calibre horses that have made it to this level usually have excellent jumping technique and take off closer to the base of the fence.

Take-off zone – and its relation to technique

A horse that is very neat with his front legs will be able comfortably to take off closer to the fence.

A horse that does not pick up his front legs so neatly will generally need to take off slightly further away, and will give the fence more height in order to clear it. These horses are often referred to as 'scopey'.

The stages of the jump from a good approach

When the approach consists of a good quality canter, maintaining balance, rhythm, impulsion and straightness, the horse is given the best opportunity to jump well. Even when the horse stands off the fence a little, or gets a little close, the quality of canter enables the horse to adjust the jump slightly in order to clear the fence. On landing, although the jump will have slightly altered the canter, it can be quickly rectified by the rider's influence, regaining rhythm, balance, impulsion and straightness. This essential aptitude means that the horse has the ability to recover, if necessary, in a double or related distance for the following jump.

Good. The horse maintains balance and rhythm throughout. The rider, however, is in front of the movement over the fence and should be looking ahead on departure.

The effects of the horse accelerating during the approach

Reasons for the canter becoming long, flat and fast:

- The canter is undeveloped because the horse is young, or the canter is not developed on the flat.
- Rider influence.
- Exuberance.
- Fear/lack of confidence.
- Rider is unable to keep the canter balanced between leg and hand.
- The horse is too fit for the work he is doing.
- Overfeeding.

When a rider feels the horse accelerate towards the fence, the natural reaction is to pull on the reins. This results in one of two outcomes: (1) the horse leans on the hand and falls on the forehand, making it difficult for him to lift up his front legs and clear the fence; or (2) he lifts his head up and hollows into the fence, which will create an inverted jump.

Often when the horse rushes, he lands deeper than he should after the fence and accelerates away. It is

Rushing. When the horse accelerates on the approach, the resulting jump is long and flat, and the horse tries to continue to accelerate on landing. This rider shows a tense, gripped position, and the horse is likely to accelerate away from the pressure.

easy to see how this could create problems in a double or a related distance, as the canter will be covering too much ground, and the horse will get too close to the second element, usually resulting in a refusal or knock-down.

A horse that rushes is more likely to take off from a long stride before the fence. Depending on the size of the fence, and scope of the horse, he will land short or long as a result. This again leads to problems during a set distance.

If the rushing horse does take off from a short point, inertia inhibits the horse's ability to lift up the front legs in time to clear the fence. He is also likely to land short or long, resulting again in difficulties at the second part of a double or related distance.

SUGGESTIONS

- Improve the quality of the canter.

- Think about the way in which your position may affect the horse.

- An exuberant horse needs to be warmed up sufficiently to use excess energy before jumping.

- A lack of confidence manifests itself in many ways. Try less demanding exercises and build confidence slowly.

- Take advice on a different bit and martingale. The bit could as easily be too strong as too mild. A horse may run through a bit that is too strong.

- Let the horse down slightly, so that he is not as fit.

- Re-assess feed.

The effects of the horse losing impulsion during the approach

Reasons for losing impulsion in the canter on the approach:

- The horse is backward thinking.
- The rider's position makes the aids ineffective.
- The horse is not in front of the leg.
- The rider takes the leg off. This sometimes happens when a rider moves into balanced position on the approach, and loses focus on maintaining impulsion.
- Fear/lack of confidence.
- Lack of focus from horse or rider.
- The horse has become sour.
- Lack of fitness.

You should aim to achieve the feeling that the horse has 'locked onto' the fence and 'takes you to the fence', maintaining the quality and rhythm of the canter. It can be very disconcerting to feel the horse back off on the approach.

If the point of take-off is good, the lack of impulsion will turn the jump into a lurch, which is not easy to remain in balance with. The horse will land short, and the effort of the jump is likely to have drained more energy. This then creates problems if in a double or related distance. Not only will the distance now be long, but the lack of impulsion will not easily be rectified.

If the take-off point is short, the horse is likely to make a very vertical hop over the fence. He will again land short, with the same problems as above.

A horse that loses impulsion on the approach is unlikely to take off from a long stride, and would prefer to put in a little short stride in front of the fence before take-off. If he does take off long, the resulting jump will feel enormous from the effort it

Lacking impulsion. The horse approaches in canter, but falls into trot immediately before the fence. The horse makes little shape over the jump, and departs with little impulsion. Notice the horse's unhappy expression. The rider is driving with her seat, and the upper body has come behind the movement. The horse finds it difficult to carry the rider in this position.

will require. Again, the horse will land short, with the same problems as above.

SUGGESTIONS

- Improve the quality of the canter and ensure that the horse is in front of the leg.

- Think of the way in which your position influences the horse.

- Develop the horse's confidence by working with less demanding exercises.

- Vary the horse's work. Inspire enthusiasm.

- Increase fitness and re-assess feed if necessary.

- Use a milder bit.

Lack of impulsion causes a short landing. This inhibits the hind legs as they follow over the jump.

SOLUTIONS

It is self-evident from these scenarios that the approach is critical to the outcome of the jump. Solutions to problems require knowledgeable instruction and dedication from the rider. With an older, established horse, the changes that you can achieve may be limited. In these cases, often the rider must adapt to the horse.

Diagnosing the source of the problem is the first step to finding a solution. Most often, the source is the quality of the canter. It is easy to underestimate the time that is required to develop the canter. It is not sufficient simply to maintain a rhythm. The horse must develop the power, suppleness and discipline in the canter to the best of his and his rider's ability in order to make improvements when jumping. The canter should continue to develop over the course of many years, as the horse becomes stronger and more adept. The next chapter offers exercises to improve the quality of canter.

2 FLATWORK FOR JUMPING

It is important that considerable time is given to improving the horse's flatwork in any discipline. A good quality canter is crucial to the jumping horse and, although jumping itself has a tendency to improve the canter, flatwork exercises can be more precise in achieving the improvement necessary.

Flatwork considerations:

- Responsiveness to the aids.
- Impulsion.
- Straightness.
- Balance and rhythm.
- Lateral and longitudinal suppleness.
- Engagement.
- Accuracy.
- Harmony between horse and rider.

The following series of exercises are designed to improve the horse's way of going. The aim is to create a more balanced, capable and athletic horse, who becomes more enjoyable and versatile to ride, and who finds jumping easier as a result.

The exercises are aimed primarily at improving the canter, and therefore assume basic correct training in the walk, trot and canter, to the standard that the horse would be able to achieve a good dressage test at high level Preliminary or lower level Novice.

1 TRANSITIONS

Every time you ride a transition, think of riding it forward. Ride from leg to hand. This is often forgotten during downward transitions, when the leg is most necessary to keep the horse balanced. Well-ridden transitions produce engagement of the horse's hindquarters, which is required in order for the horse to propel himself up and over a jump.

Exercise 1(a)

- Ride a transition from trot to walk at every other letter in the school. Walk for a few steps, and then trot on again.

- Ride the same exercise at every letter.

- Ride a direct transition from trot – halt – trot at every other letter.

CONSIDER – the rider's position and preparation, responsiveness to the aids, and accuracy.

Repeat until the horse becomes rhythmical and balanced throughout.

Exercise 1(b)

- On a 20m circle, repeat transitions to and from canter, aiming for greater balance and responsiveness each time.

- Canter one complete circle, trot half a circle. Repeat.

- Ride the same exercise, making direct upwards transitions from walk to canter, and downwards if you are able. If not, make progressive downward transitions through trot, to walk. Maintain the quality and rhythm of each pace through the transitions.

CONSIDER – position, preparation, responsiveness, accuracy, balance and rhythm, especially during the downward transitions.

2 END OF WARM-UP EXERCISE

Once the horse has been warmed up to loosen the muscles and you start to ask him to work with greater use of his hindquarters and a slightly shorter frame, this is a useful exercise to help you to achieve engagement.

- Ride a 20m square.

- Ride the sides of the square in trot, and make a transition to walk, just before every corner, to ride the corners in walk.

- When riding through the corners, think of controlling the horse's shoulders through the turn using your outside aids.

- Return to trot once you have ridden out of the corner.

This is a mentally demanding exercise on both horse and rider. The rider must constantly be preparing for the following transition, as the size of the exercise does not allow the rider to be inattentive. If the rider communicates to the horse well, the horse will

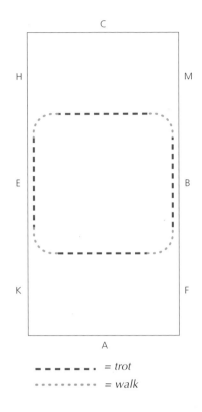

= trot
= walk

quickly become more responsive.

Jumping requires rapid mental preparation, accuracy and co-ordination of the aids. This exercise should improve the rider's ability to ride balanced turns during the approach to and departure from a fence.

3 FIGURE-OF-EIGHT

A horse that lacks lateral suppleness should have plenty of circle work included in his training. The rider should aim for the horse to be able to canter evenly on both reins, taking the same number of strides on each circle and maintaining the same rhythm.

- Work to achieve a rhythmical canter on one circle.

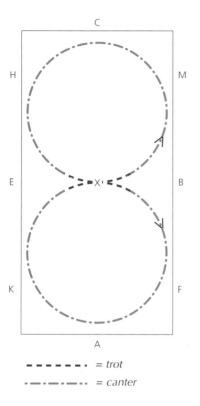

= trot

= canter

This exercise can be directly related to riding a course, during which, the rider may be required to change the horse's canter lead through trot. The rhythm of the canter must then immediately be re-established for the course to flow.

4 THREE-LOOP SERPENTINE

Develop this exercise in exactly the same way as the previous one.

The serpentine is more demanding than the last exercise because the turns are more acute and the transitions occur more quickly. This exercise illustrates the control required to make balanced and rhythmical turns in the canter, such as may be found in a jump-off course.

- Make a change of lead leg through trot, as if on a figure-of-eight, onto the opposite rein and circle.

- Work to achieve a rhythmical canter on this circle.

- Once the rhythm is achieved on the second circle, return to the original circle, again through a change of lead leg through trot.

- Repeat the exercise until you are able to ride a continuous figure-of-eight, immediately returning to the rhythm of the canter after the change of lead leg through trot.

- Try to develop the exercise so that you ride a simple change (canter–walk–canter) to change the canter lead. This direct transition will further help the horse's engagement.

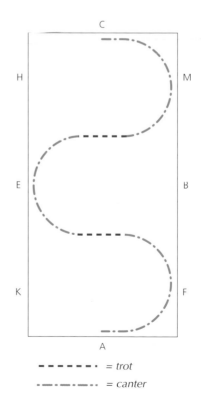

= trot

= canter

5 INCREASING AND DECREASING THE SIZE OF A CIRCLE

This exercise helps to improve rhythm, balance, engagement and lateral suppleness of the horse.

• Canter on a 20m circle. Establish rhythm and balance.

• Decrease the size of the circle to 15m. The rhythm and balance should remain the same. If it does not, work to improve by increasing and decreasing the size of the circle between 20m and 15m. Regain the balance and rhythm on the 20m circle and gradually decrease to 15m. Be acutely aware of when, and therefore why, you lose the rhythm, to enable you to work to improve it. Rhythm may be lost due to a loss of:

  • balance
  • straightness

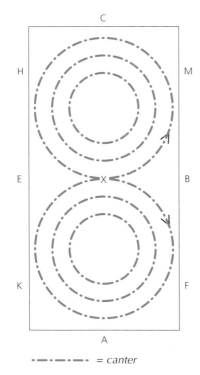

= canter

• impulsion.
• bend
• rider's position
• connection between leg and hand

• Repeat on the other rein.

• Once the horse can maintain the rhythm between 20m and 15m circles, work towards decreasing the circle to 10m.

• Count the number of strides on each size circle on both reins. Firstly, the number should be the same on both reins. This would suggest that the horse is even on both reins. Secondly, there should be an obvious relationship between the 20m, 15m and 10m circles regarding the number of strides on each.

Working to maintain the rhythm on smaller circles will help the rider to maintain the rhythm through each turn to a fence.

6 MAINTAINING THE RHYTHM IN THE CANTER

Riding a rhythmical course should be an aim for all. Working to maintain rhythm on the flat will improve the rider's ability to recognise when and why it is lost when jumping.

• In canter, ride large around the school.

• Whenever the rhythm is lost, ride a 10m–15m circle, depending on the ability of the horse and rider to regain it. The danger areas of the school are:

(1) the long sides, where the horse can become long and flat, and

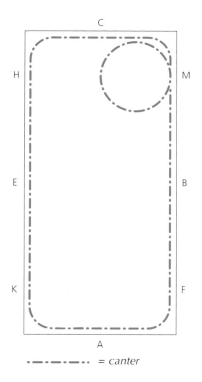

—·—·—·—·· = *canter*

rider becomes aware of where the rhythm could potentially be lost, the more he will be able to ride positively to maintain it.

7 LENGTHENING AND SHORTENING THE STRIDE

The horse must learn to shorten and lengthen the stride while maintaining the rhythm, in order to be able to vary the stride-length, if necessary during a course. A good jumping horse has versatility in his canter.

Exercise 7(a)

- In working canter, on a 20m circle, count the number of strides taken on one complete circle.

- Shorten the canter and again count the number of

(2) the corners, where the horse is likely to lose balance.

- Work towards being able to maintain the rhythm, balance and impulsion of the canter at all times, and to recognise when you are about to lose it. In this way, you can work to maintain the canter, rather than correcting it once it is lost.

- Once the rhythm has been established going large on the track, repeat the exercise on an inner track. On the inner track, the boards will not support the horse, and therefore the rider must work harder with the outside aids.

This seemingly simple exercise teaches the rider to feel when the rhythm of the horse is lost. By fine-tuning awareness, the rider should be able to prevent the loss occurring. Every jumping exercise will consist of turns and straight lines. The more the

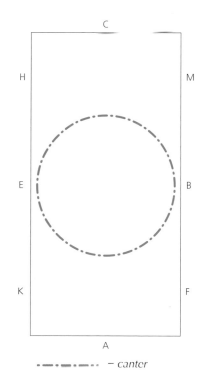

—·—·—·—·· – *canter*

strides during one complete circle. Try to feel that you are maintaining the rhythm by riding positively from leg to hand, and shortening the frame of the horse, rather than slowing the canter down by using the rein only. Reciting the days of the week in the rhythm of your working canter may help you to maintain the rhythm of your shortened canter. If the canter feels precious, as if it could fall into trot at any moment, you know that you need more leg.

- Lengthen the canter, and repeat the counting. Again, work to keep the rhythm, and do not allow the canter to fall onto the forehand. If that happens, the horse will become heavy in the hand and the canter long and flat.

- If, when varying the stride for a whole circle, the horse does lose rhythm, shorten and lengthen for

half a circle at a time, and gradually build up to one complete circle.

Exercise 7(b)

- Ride the threequarter line in canter and find two markers that you can use to count the strides in between.

- Ride to shorten and lengthen the stride to determine how many strides you can fit in, while maintaining the rhythm.

- When lengthening, the horse is more likely to lose the rhythm on a straight line than he is on a circle. The shape of the circle helps to keep the horse connected.

Both these exercises help the rider to develop the ability to shorten and lengthen the canter while maintaining the rhythm. This is useful on the approach to any fence, especially when riding through a related distance.

8 ASKING FOR A SPECIFIC CANTER LEAD AT VARIOUS POINTS IN THE SCHOOL

The sequence of footfalls in the canter, and how to recognise the canter lead, is covered in Chapter 8 – Influencing the Canter Lead.

- Make a transition to canter, using the correct aids in corners and on circles.

- Ask for the correct leading leg along the long sides of the school. If the horse is confused, leg yield from the threequarter line to the track, and at the moment you reach the track, ask for canter.

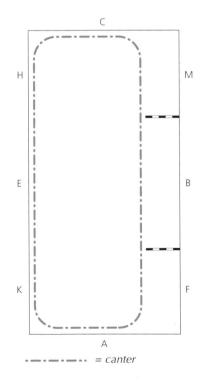

· — · — · · = canter

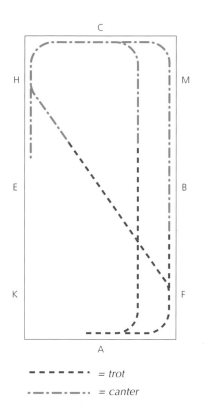

----- = trot

.—.—.—.. = canter

9 CANTERING A SHALLOW LOOP

The straightness of a horse can be improved through the use of counter-canter. Cantering a shallow loop is the first exercise that is taught to horse and rider when introducing counter-canter. It develops in the rider an awareness of the horse's balance in canter.

- Ride 5m shallow loops in trot.

- Moving into canter, work to achieve balance and rhythm on 20m circles and going large.

- Once balance and rhythm are established ride a 1–2m shallow loop along the long side of the school. In the trot, the bend of the horse changes with the shape of the loop. In the canter, the bend of the horse must remain over the lead leg of the

You must prepare for the transition during the leg yielding. Leg yielding moves the horse from the inside leg into the outside rein, making it clearer to the horse on which lead to strike off.

- Repeat on the opposite rein.

- Once the horse is more confident in the exercise, ask for specific leads in less obvious areas – on the threequarter line or across the long diagonal (ensure that the horse remains on a straight line with both of these exercises).

During a course, the rider may wish to change canter leads. There may not always be a convenient corner in which to do this, and therefore the rider must train the horse to respond to the correct aids, anywhere that the canter is asked for.

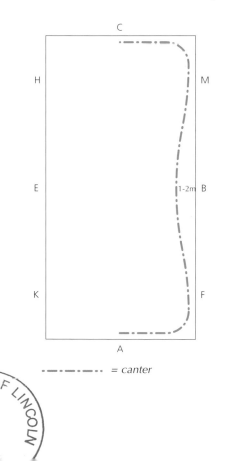

.—.—.—.. = canter

horse. This means that from the deepest part of the loop, on the return to the track, the horse is in counter-canter – i.e. he is moving in the opposite direction to his bend.

- Once the loop has been ridden, ride a 20m circle at the opposite end of the school to regain any balance and rhythm that has been lost. Repeat on the other rein.

- Once the rider has developed the co-ordination and feel to maintain the horse's balance on the 1–2m loops, then the loops can gradually be increased in depth. The horse will also develop his balance during the exercise, and should improve in straightness.

This exercise also has practical implications for manoeuvring the horse around jumps when necessary.

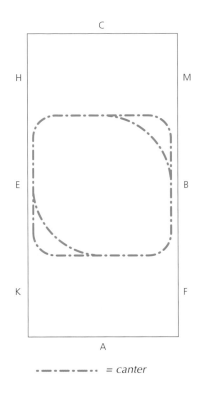

 = canter

10 CANTERING A SQUARE

The shape of the square requires the rider to turn the horse's shoulders around each corner. At that moment, the horse is carrying more weight on his hind legs, and thus the horse should become more engaged from riding the exercise. This should result in an improvement in the quality of the canter.

- Ride a 20m square, firstly in walk and then in trot. Pay particular attention to the corners. Have the feeling that you are bringing the shoulders of the horse around in front of the quarters by using the outside aids – outside leg to hand.

- You are not aiming to ride a pirouette (turn on the haunches) at each corner, but the thought of a pirouette will help you to bring the shoulders

around. Ensure that the bend remains to the inside and that your legs maintain the rhythm.

- When the horse and rider have developed the feel in the walk and trot, develop the exercise into the canter. If the exercise occurs too rapidly for the rider to manage, ride only the two opposite corners, and let the others be rounded, as if on a circle.

- Repeat on both reins.

This exercise should help the rider to improve the way in which turns to fences are ridden. Having the thought of moving the horse's shoulders through a turn gives the rider far greater ability to control the horse and helps to maintain balance and rhythm.

11 RIDING A COURSE ON THE FLAT

Armed with the knowledge and improvements that should have developed from the previous exercises, make up a simple course mentally.

- Ride the course firstly in trot.

- If you lose the rhythm, balance, impulsion or straightness at any time, walk, try to determine why, and repeat to improve. Whatever problems occur in the trot will become exaggerated in the canter, so it is worth putting in the effort during the trot stage, before moving onto the canter.

- Canter the exercise. Work to maintain the balance, rhythm, impulsion and straightness. Change the horse's canter lead as necessary.

This is a valuable exercise, as the rider can concentrate on the business of course riding without any concerns for the jumps.

3 EFFECTS OF THE RIDER'S POSITION

There is no greater feeling of harmony between horse and rider than that experienced during those moments when riding feels effortless. This is why so many riders strive to achieve perfection in their position. Only when the rider is able to carry himself in a balanced, secure and harmonious position is the horse able to achieve the graceful athleticism of his potential.

For the jumping rider, achieving a correct position will enable you to:

- Remain in balance with the horse during the approach, take-off, jump, landing and departure.

- Positively influence the horse.

- Develop security for personal stability.

- Develop confidence, and therefore help to develop the horse's confidence.

- Become adaptable to any horse ridden.

1 TAKING BALANCED POSITION

- The length of stirrup will depend on your physique, but you should aim to have a 90° bend at the knee when sitting in the saddle, with your heel down.

- Allow the weight to drop through your heel, so that the heel is slightly lower than your toe, but without pushing the lower leg forwards.

- Open the knee slightly to allow the lower leg to wrap around the horse's sides. Your security comes from the lower leg, not from the knee. If you learn to grip with the knee, the lower leg becomes insecure and you are then vulnerable and ineffective.

- Push your seat slightly further back in the saddle, allowing your upper body to fold forwards from the hips. Keep the back straight.

- Shorten the reins to compensate for the fact that your hands will move forwards as your upper body folds forwards.

- Raise your seat off the saddle so that there is a small layer of air between your seat and the saddle.

- You should now have a straight vertical line through your ear, shoulder, knee and toe.

- Your centre of gravity flows through the ball of your foot and heel.

- Your hips, knees and ankles will absorb the movement of the horse.

'Balanced position' is used within this book to describe the position adopted when jumping. It is also known as jumping position, forward seat and light seat.

This position illustrates balance and harmony with the horse. The rider carries weight through her heel, and displays a secure lower leg. She is neither ahead nor behind the movement, but in an ideal position to move in balance with the horse's flight over the fence. Her back is straight, allowing her to have control over her upper body. Both the rider and the horse are focused ahead. The rider's arms are relaxed, allowing a good 'crest-release', while maintaining a light, non-restrictive contact on the horse's mouth.

IMPROVING YOUR BALANCED POSITION ON THE FLAT

Before embarking on jumping, try to make yourself as versatile at riding in balanced position as you are in your flatwork position. Not only will this develop your security, balance and feel within your balanced position, but it will also offer you an alternative position in which to ride the canter in between the fences during a course. This may help you to develop more rhythm in the canter.

Exercises to be ridden in balanced position:

- School figures in walk, trot and canter.
- Transition, both progressive and direct.
- Leg yielding.
- Lengthening and shortening the stride.
- Hacking – especially over undulating land. This will require you to alter your position slightly in order to remain in balance with the horse, and to

maintain the rhythm. For example, when riding downhill, lift the shoulders up slightly to remain in balance and to prevent the horse from increasing in pace and falling on the forehand.

2 HOW TO MAINTAIN BALANCE WITH THE HORSE OVER THE FENCE

A secure and balanced position lays the foundation for a rider to be able to maintain balance and security as the horse jumps.

- When the horse jumps, the rider must learn, through repetition, to move with the horse and remain in balance. This is best learned on a horse that will make a jump over small fences, as the movement of the horse's jump will be less.

This young rider is showing a good 'crest release' by running her hands up the pony's neck to allow him to stretch.

- Keep the weight in the heel, with a soft knee and secure lower leg.

- As the horse jumps, allow your upper body to move with the jump, while keeping a straight back and looking ahead.

- Over a small fence, the jump of the horse will feel less dramatic than over a larger one. The larger the fence, the more the horse will stretch his head and neck forwards, and therefore the more the rider will need to learn to give with his hands. The aim is to maintain a light feel of the horse's mouth over the fence, so that the rider has neither dropped the contact completely, nor is restrictive.

- When learning to jump, you will be taught to hold onto a section of the horse's mane as well as the reins. This will prevent you from pulling on the reins as you learn to feel the movement. Once you are able to move with the horse, holding the mane will no longer be necessary, and you will learn to allow your hands forwards as the horse stretches his head and neck over the fence, known as the 'crest release'.

This rider's position shows security and balance with the horse over the jump.

A secure and correct position during take-off.

- As the horse starts his descent from the jump, the rider's upper body should automatically lift the shoulders up to remain in balance, similarly to hacking downhill in balanced position. The rider must ensure that he does not allow his seat to drop back into the saddle. If the rider stays forwards as the horse descends, this will cause the horse to land with too much weight on the forehand, making it difficult for the horse to recover his balance and canter on landing.

In balance with the horse on landing.

- The impact of landing is absorbed through the rider's hips, knees and ankles.

3 WHEN THE RIDER BECOMES AHEAD OF THE MOVEMENT

What happens

- The heels rise and the lower leg moves back, losing the rider's security.

- The knee grips, inhibiting the movement of the horse's shoulders.

This rider's position is ahead of the movement.

- The upper body tips forwards.

- The rider leans on his hands.

- The rider's centre of gravity is in front of the foot.

During the jump

- The rider's weight is suddenly in front of the horse as the horse jumps, making it more of an effort for the horse to lift up his shoulders. This often results in the horse taking the fence down with the front legs.

- The heel rises, the knee becomes tight.

- The rider's seat may move in front of the pommel of the saddle and the rider appears to be over the neck of the horse

- The horse lands on the forehand because the rider's weight is too far forwards. The canter is unbalanced after the fence, usually long, flat and accelerating.

Reasons for this happening

- An insecure position.

- The rider makes too much effort over the fence.

- The horse backs off the fence, or loses impulsion on the approach, causing the rider to become ahead of the movement in an effort to commit the horse.

Corrections

- Work to improve security in the position.

- Wait for the horse to jump, and only move as much as is necessary.

- Have the horse in front of the leg and travelling forwards to the fence.

- Commit the horse to the fence with your legs.

4 WHEN THE RIDER GETS BEHIND THE MOVEMENT

What happens

- Too much weight in the heel and insecurity in the lower leg causes the lower leg to slip forwards.

- The upper body moves behind the vertical.

- The seat sits in the saddle.

- The reins become too long.

- The rider's centre of gravity is behind the foot.

This rider has been left behind the movement.

During the jump

- The rider's bodyweight is behind the movement of the horse as he jumps.

- The lower leg slips forwards causing the seat to sit in the saddle. This is sufficient to drop the horse's hind legs into the fence.

- The upper body comes back, causing the rider to pull on the reins and restrict the horse.

- On landing, the horse may run away from the pressure, or have lost all impulsion. Either way, the rhythm of the canter is lost.

Reasons for this happening

- The rider tries too hard to push the heel down, and as a result, the lower leg swings forwards.

- Apprehension about jumping – the rider is not committed.

- The horse takes off before the rider is expecting it.

- Defensive riding – the rider is used to riding horses that refuse. Ironically, this is a vicious circle. The more uncomfortable the horse is, the less likely he is to jump.

Corrections

- Improve balance and security in the position.

- Take balanced position before the fence. This way, you are more prepared to jump with the horse.

- If nervous of jumping, seek instruction to develop confidence.

5 THE RIDER IS TIGHT WITH THE REINS OVER THE FENCE

While working the horse in balanced position it is essential to maintain a contact on the horse's mouth. However, when a horse jumps, he needs full use of his neck for several functions:

- Balance.

- To enable him to lift up through the shoulders and bring up the forelegs.

- To enable his back to round over the fence to produce the shape known as the 'bascule'. When the back is allowed to be supple, the horse can lift up the hind legs to follow the shape.

- On landing, the horse uses his head and neck to balance into the departure.

What happens

- The process described above is restricted.

Tightness with the reins over the fence.

During the jump

- The horse is unable to stretch his head and neck forwards, which restricts the shoulders, back and hind legs.

- The horse may have the fence down with the front, or most commonly the hind legs.

- If the rider seriously restricts the horse, he may refuse.

Reasons for this happening

- The rider is behind the movement and pulls on the reins for support.

- The rider does not soften the hands over the fence

- The rider tries to 'pick the horse up' with his hands over the fence.

- The rider feels the horse accelerate into the fence and is still pulling as the horse jumps. See Chapter 5 - Overcoming Problems.

Corrections

- Develop balance and security in the position.

- Hold on to the mane as the horse jumps until you feel balanced and confident enough to begin to soften your hands.

- Accept that it is the rider's responsibility to produce a canter in balance and rhythm, and to maintain a good position, but it is the horse's responsibility to jump the fence. Do not try to pick the horse up with your hands!

6 THE RIDER WHO IS TOO QUICK IN THE AIR

The role of the rider when the horse is in the air over a fence is an active or passive one depending on how you view it:

- It is active in the sense that you actively want to achieve balance and harmony with your horse, and allow him to jump as naturally as possible.

- It is passive in the sense that you want the position to remain quiet so that it does not negatively influence or restrict the horse's jump.

What happens

- The rider snaps forwards and snaps back with his upper body over the fence, rather than gently staying in harmony with the horse.

Quickness of the rider's position has not given the horse time to relax and make a better shape over the fence.

During the jump

If a rider is quick with his position, it influences the horse to become quick in its jump. This can result in the horse becoming:

- Flat over the fence.

- Hollow over the fence.

- Tight over the back and therefore not following through cleanly with the hind legs.

- Unable to bring up the front or hind legs quickly enough.

- Influenced to be quick on landing and therefore accelerating away from the fence.

- Lacking in confidence, leading to refusals and run-outs.

Reasons for this happening

- The rider who sits and drives with the seat on the approach, is often positioned behind the movement. Because the rider is so far back with the upper body, he learns to be quick and snap forwards as the horse jumps, and then becomes quick to snap back after the fence and once more drive with his seat.

- The rider has not learned to feel the movement of the horse jumping, and as a result moves robotically.

- The rider has learned to ride on a horse or pony with a quick jump. This can often be noticed when a child moves from quick, nippy ponies onto horses.

Sitting and driving with the seat on the approach to a fence. The horse's unhappy expression says it all.

Corrections

- Try never to drive from the seat. Your legs generate energy from the horse's hind legs. Make the horse responsive to the aids and have him in front of the leg during warm-up.

- Take lessons to develop the feel of moving with the horse correctly over the fence.

The rider sits heavily during landing, making it difficult for the horse to follow through with his hind legs.

7 THE RIDER SITS IN THE SADDLE WHILE THE HORSE IS JUMPING

The aim for any rider over any fence is to allow the horse the freedom to jump.

What happens

- The rider sits up early and lands on the horse's back.

During the jump

- The horse may hollow – the horse's head comes up, the back becomes tight, and the hind legs are dropped in the fence.

- The rider may sit up a fraction too soon and just touch the saddle. This may be sufficient to make the horse clip the back rail with his hind legs.

Reasons for this happening

- Lack of confidence in the rider.

- Insecurity of the lower leg, forcing the rider to compensate with the upper body to remain in balance.

Corrections

- Seek instruction to gain confidence.

- Develop security in your position.

- Absorb the movement on landing through the knees, ankles and hips.

8 THE RIDER WHO LEANS TO THE LEFT/RIGHT OVER A FENCE

What happens

- While in the air, the rider leans to one side.

During the jump

- The horse loses balance and straightness.

- The movement of the rider influences the horse to jump to the side.

- The horse is unbalanced on landing.

Reasons for this happening

- The rider is crooked.

- The stirrups are not level. Many riders become used to riding with odd-length stirrups but feel as if they are level.

- The rider is looking to one side to see the leading leg on landing, or in an effort to influence the lead leg over the fence. See Chapter 8 – Influencing the Canter Lead.

- The rider is looking at the next fence and in so doing has moved his body, rather than just his head.

Corrections

- Correct your position on the flat first. Taking regular lunge lessons will help to improve your position.

The rider is leaning to one side to assess the lead leg. She risks unbalancing the horse.

- Try to learn to feel the leading leg. If you do need to look, try to allow only your eyes to glance down.

- Looking at the following fence is essential, but try to turn your head only, and not let your body lean.

Each rider has a slightly different physical shape. Whatever your shape or size, practising under instruction will help you to develop a secure and balanced position, which, in turn, will allow the horse the freedom of movement to jump to the best of his ability.

FENCES TO IMPROVE THE HORSE'S TECHNIQUE

The ideal jumping horse has many qualities:

- a desire to jump and not touch a fence
- trainability
- good jumping technique
- bravery
- good conformation

The previous chapters have shown the stages of jumping and the effects of the rider's position. This chapter aims to show how the horse's technique over a fence and the bascule (the shape that the horse makes over a fence) can be improved by using different types of fence.

Ground poles, including trot and canter poles, aid the horse to maintain a rhythm on the approach to and departure from a fence. The horse must be able to maintain a rhythm to the fence in order for the fence to improve the horse's technique. See Chapter 6 – Polework.

1 CROSS-POLES

When building cross-poles, place the ends of the poles on either side of the wings. This enables the fence to be jumped from either direction.

A high-sided cross-pole is difficult for the horse to jump, as the lowest part of the jump, the centre, is narrow. The resulting jump will be higher than expected in order for the horse to clear it.

Used for

- Introduction to jumping for the young horse or inexperienced rider.

- Teaching the horse and rider to aim for the centre of the fence.

- Warming up for jumping.

- Used as the first fence at the start of a grid as it is

Simple cross-pole.

A cross-pole helps horse and rider to aim for the centre.

an inviting fence, channelling the horse to the centre of the grid.

Used to correct

- A horse that tends to jump to one side over fences. Using a series of cross-poles, firstly as a grid, developing into a course, you can encourage the horse to maintain straightness. The size of the fence(s) needs to be built up gradually so that it is relatively steep-sided, approximately 3ft 3ins (1m) at each side, which makes the 'V' shape formed more exaggerated, and therefore more effective.

2 VERTICALS

When building a vertical, you need to include a ground line. This can be a simple pole at the base of the fence on the approach side. With verticals over 2ft (60cm), a ground line such as this can make the fence look a little 'gappy', so either a filler or other poles should be included so that the fence is 'filled in' a little more. The alternative is to use a 'hanger'. This is a pole that is positioned diagonally under the fence. The position of the base of the hanger can

determine from which direction the fence should be jumped. The base of the hanger should meet the ground on the approach side of the jump. A hanger whose base is directly under the fence allows the vertical to be jumped from either direction.

Used for

- Encouraging the horse to become neater with his front legs.

- Encouraging more engagement of the hind legs to propel the horse upwards.

- The vertical needs to be of sufficient size to create a good jumping effort to show improvement in the horse's technique. The size used will depend upon the level of training of the horse.

Used to correct

- A horse that tends to make a flat shape over the fence.

The quality of the canter will need to be improved so that the horse is able to have sufficient contained power to use his hind legs to propel himself up and let the fence help him to become neater with his

Vertical, one direction. Note hanger position.

Vertical, both directions.

Neat front legs. A vertical encourages the horse to improve front-leg technique.

forelegs. If the canter is long and flat, then inevitably, the jump will be long and flat. This can be confidence-sapping for the horse.

- When placed within a grid, related distance or after canter poles, the use of verticals is likely to show the greatest improvement, as the take-off

This combination of cross-pole and vertical encourages straightness over a fence.

point is regulated.

- A combination of a vertical and a cross-pole (in one fence) can aid a horse to maintain straightness.

3 SPREADS

Spreads can be made ascending, parallel, or from two cross-poles:

An **ascending spread** must only ever be jumped by approaching from the lower side. An ascending spread may consist of a cross-pole in front, with a vertical behind, or two vertical poles, the front rail being lower than the back. If comprised of two verticals, the front rail will need a ground line.

A **parallel** is built so that the front and back rails are the same height. If intended to be jumped in one direction only, the ground line can be positioned at the front. If the fence is required to be jumped from both directions, there needs to be a ground line on both sides.

Ascending spread.

A parallel to be jumped from one direction. The hanger is at the front of the fence.

With hangers on both sides, this parallel can be jumped from either direction.

A **spread of two cross-poles** can be ascending, or of the same height.

Used for

- Encouraging the horse to stretch as he jumps.

- An ascending spread is an inviting fence and should be used to introduce spreads to a horse.

- The use of a cross-pole in an ascending spread encourages straightness.

- A parallel combines the effect of the vertical and the spread. The front and back rails of the fence are built at the same height. A parallel helps the horse to produce good front-leg technique. Parallels also develop athleticism in the jump by encouraging more power from the hind legs and suppleness in the back, as the horse pushes off the ground to stretch over the width of the fence.

A spread will encourage a horse to stretch.

Used to correct

- A horse that tends to jump vertically, i.e. straight up and down with no width to the jump. This type of horse tends to have a short, bouncy canter and is often very neat over a vertical. In order for the horse to clear a spread, the horse must be taught to make the canter bigger and more forward, while maintaining rhythm and balance – flatwork first.

Introduction of spreads to improve the jump should start with ascending spreads, as the horse will find it easier initially to improve the jump using these.

4 A-FRAMES

Introducing A-frames

- For the A-frame to improve the horse's technique, the take-off point must be accurate. For this reason, either approach the A-frame out of trot or canter, using a placing pole, or use it within a grid of two elements, the A-frame as the second element, approaching the first element from trot.

- The A-frame is most commonly built with a vertical so, when warming up, start by jumping a vertical and progress to making it into an A-frame.

- The A-frame must be built gradually. Introduce it by placing a pole on either end of the fence, from the vertical to the ground, ensuring always that it remains wider at the ground than it is at the fence. Once the horse is showing confidence, you can progress to the next step.

- Gradually move the poles into the centre of the fence, so that eventually the ends of the poles are touching in the centre of the vertical. Do not allow the point of the inverted 'V' to be higher than absolutely necessary.

Used for

- Encouraging the horse to use his shoulders and come up through the withers and therefore become neater with his front legs.

- Developing looseness through the back.

- Developing a good follow-through with the hind legs.

- Straightness.

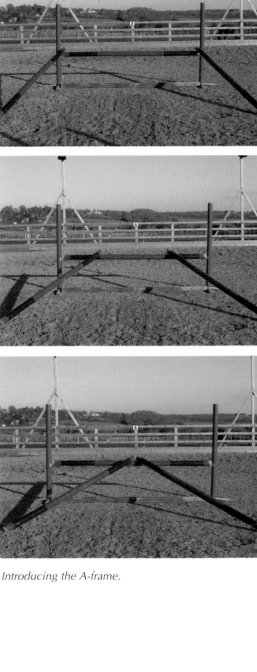

Introducing the A-frame.

TOP: *Many young horses start with a loose front leg technique.*
CENTRE: *Using an A-frame can teach the horse to use himself in a better way over the fence.*
BOTTOM: *Having removed the A-frame, the horse retains his knowledge and is neater in front than in the first photo.*
NB: *The rider's position is a little ahead of the movement.*

Used to correct

- A horse that does not lift up through the shoulders and is 'dangly' with his front legs.

- A horse that tends not to use his back, and often has fences down with his hind legs.

5 FILLERS

Introduction of fillers

Many horses are very accepting of the obstacles that we ask them to jump, but it is nevertheless very important in the early stages of a horse's jump training that time is taken to introduce him to potentially scary fence fillers. If a horse is worried about fillers, then allowing him the time to develop confidence slowly will save you countless hours in the future – and if he learns to take on fillers boldly, the time spent in his education is of no cost.

- Work on the flat around the fillers. Gauge the horse's response. If he takes no notice, then he is likely not to worry when you ask him to jump them. If he shows signs of anxiety, continue with the flatwork until he is relaxed. At the end of the session, walk him over to the fillers and allow him to investigate them if he wishes. This should convince him that there are no hidden monsters.

- When it comes to introducing the fillers into a jump, select the smallest ones to work with.

- Place a filler on either side of a vertical fence as a funnel. The vertical should be a little higher than the fillers, so that the fillers can be slotted in underneath. Look up on your approach, keep the horse between leg and hand, and ride positively. Jump the fence until the horse is unconcerned about the fillers and showing confidence.

- Gradually move the fillers into position, reducing the gap between them, until the fillers are positioned correctly in the fence line. Do not rush this step. Be sure to wait until the horse is confident before moving the fillers closer.

- It should not be necessary to introduce each filler to the horse in this way. Once the horse is confident over one or two sets of fillers, the rest should be jumped positively as normal fences. Although it's debatable whether horses see in colour, sometimes one particular colour can become an issue. If this is the case, invest in fillers of this colour, or repaint old ones, and work the horse with them as if introducing fillers for the first time.

Used for

- Training competition horses – fillers need to be introduced to every competitive horse as they are found in virtually every competition.

Introducing fillers progressively.

Used to correct

- A horse that rushes can be encouraged to back off a fence by including a filler.

- A horse that is flat as he jumps may be encouraged to make a better shape by building a filler into the fence.

New fillers often encourage the horse to give more height and a better shape over the fence.

5 SOLVING PROBLEMS

Almost every horse, with gradual, correct training, enjoys jumping. Those with a big heart and courage will endeavour to do their best for sympathetic riders and they often achieve a much higher standard than their talent would initially lead you to believe.

Problems, if they occur, frequently derive from a lack of either confidence or correct training. It is important, therefore, that no matter how frustrating an issue becomes, the rider and trainer must endeavour to find a constructive solution. This is the way to build a confident, trusting and respectful partnership between horse and rider. Some issues may be easily resolved independently, but it never hurts to seek advice from a knowledgeable person.

In the following examples, it is assumed that the horse is in good physical health and is receiving routine inspections regarding back, worming, teeth and shoeing. It is also assumed that the tack fits and causes no discomfort, and that the horse is fed correctly for the workload.

1 THE HORSE RUSHES TOWARDS FENCES

Riding a horse that tries to take control and runs towards every fence can be a very unnerving experience. Often a fight ensues between horse and rider on the way into the fence, and this usually results in a less than perfect jump.

POSSIBLE REASONS

(a) Fear.

(b) Exuberance.

(c) The horse is opinionated.

(d) Rider's position.

(e) Rider's fear.

(f) The bit is too strong/not strong enough.

(g) 'Firing the horse'.

(a) Fear

If the horse is frightened of a jump, he will follow

Accelerating towards the fence.

his natural instinct and run. If the rider is capable of keeping the horse straight, this means that the horse will rush at the fence to jump the obstacle as quickly as possible, whereas with a rider of less ability, you may find that the horse will run out of the fence.

CORRECTIONS

If a horse has developed a fear of jumping, take the schooling back a couple of stages, and build up again slowly.

If a new fence has been introduced, such as a water tray or planks, and is now causing problems, look at the way in which it was introduced. You may now need to spend time riding on the flat around the fence, before gradually building the horse's confidence to jump a very small version of the jump. When schooling, it is important to finish a session on a good note.

(b) Exuberance

A naturally exuberant horse can be a joy to work if managed correctly. An exuberant type, incorrectly managed, could be potentially lethal when jumping, as he could take the fences on with little regard for his own or his rider's safety.

CORRECTIONS

The management of an intelligent horse is very important:

- Make his work varied and interesting.

- Stable him in a busier area of the yard – give him something to watch.

- Include turn-out time with companions.

- Possibly work him more than once a day.

- Warm him up sufficiently so that excess energy is used before jumping.

- Ride jumping exercises that require discipline.

- Be consistent with his training.

(c) The horse is opinionated

Some horses think they know better than their riders and try to take control.

CORRECTIONS

You must ensure that your decisions are correct. Sometimes a seemingly opinionated horse is actually making the right decisions, while the rider is wrong. Also understand that an older, established horse has learned to jump in a particular way. It may be very difficult to instigate a change, and the rider may indeed need to become adaptable to the horse in order to maintain the horse's confidence.

Opinionated.

- Work to instil discipline in the flat work. If the horse accepts the rider's control on the flat, you have more chance of carrying this over into the jumping.

- When jumping, never give up over any issue that you truly feel is correct. For example, if schooling around a course of fences, insist that the horse maintains his rhythm into every fence. If the rhythm is lost, circle to regain it and repeat until you approach in the way you want. Finish the session on this positive note. Remember here that a Thoroughbred type generally becomes agitated with repetition. So to achieve success you may need to change the exercise, work for a short time on the flat, or even lunge the horse, before returning to the exercise. Ensure that good work is positively reinforced with lots of praise!

(d) Rider's position

Is the rider:

- in front of the movement?

- leaning back and driving with the seat?

- worrying the horse with an insecure lower leg?

The rider's position will affect the approach, take-off, jump, landing and departure.

CORRECTIONS

Work to improve your position. See Chapter 3 – Effects of the Rider's Position.

(e) Rider's fear

A nervous rider transmits fear through tension in his body, communicating it to the horse. This will often make a backward-thinking horse slow down, and a forward-thinking one rush.

CORRECTIONS

- Gain confidence at a level that you are happy with.

- Choose a sympathetic instructor.

- Make gradual steps towards your goal, and remain at that level until you are very confident.

You will often find that by taking the pressure off yourself, the fear lessens and you actually make more progress.

(f) The bit is too strong/not strong enough

A horse that rushes may have a bit that is too mild to allow the rider control. Equally, horses have been known to run through a bit that is too strong in an attempt to evade the pressure.

CORRECTIONS

As a general rule, start with the mildest bit and work up through the levels until you find one that suits. You may find that using a martingale with the bit that you are currently using offers you that little extra control and that you do not need to try a stronger bit.

Take advice from a knowledgeable person regarding bitting.

(g) 'Firing the horse'

Riders are often seen holding the horse back on the approach to a fence. When the rider 'sees the stride', they kick hard, drive with their seat and lose the contact. This is termed 'firing' the horse at the fence, and breaks every rule of consistency that we aim for. It also teaches the horse to rush at the fences and tends to result in a flat jump.

CORRECTIONS

Change the way in which the horse is ridden to the fence, aiming to maintain balance and rhythm consistently. Keep the horse between leg and hand, and generate energy through use of the legs, keeping the seat quiet.

2 THE HORSE LOSES IMPULSION ON THE APPROACH TO FENCES

The ideal feeling for a rider approaching a fence should be that the horse has 'locked onto' the fence and 'takes the rider to the fence' in balance and rhythm. A horse that loses impulsion, for whatever reason, on the approach to a fence does not give the rider a feeling of confidence or enthusiasm.

POSSIBLE REASONS

(a) Lack of rider/horse fitness.

(b) The horse is backward-thinking.

(c) The rider's position.

(d) The rider's fear.

(e) Over-facing the horse.

(f) The bit is too strong.

(a) Lack of rider/horse fitness

A horse that lacks the fitness to perform the required

task is unsafe to jump.

If the rider lacks fitness, he will not be able to respond immediately to a situation and therefore could also be unsafe. The rider owes it to the horse to be fit. An unfit rider becomes a heavy burden for the horse to carry.

CORRECTION

• Gradually increase the fitness levels of horse and rider.

(b) The horse is backward-thinking

When ridden, the horse should be in front of the leg at all times – a feat that is not always easy, especially if you own a horse that does not think forwards naturally.

CORRECTIONS

• Improve the flatwork first, so that you are able to ride the horse forward in a more positive way. See Chapter 2 – Flatwork for Jumping.

• When warming up to jump include many transitions, shortening and lengthening of the stride, and sufficient canter so that he is awake

Losing impulsion.

and forward, but not tired.

- Vary his work to keep him interested.

- Improve his general fitness

(c) The rider's position

If the position is weak and lacks security, the rider may be unable to use the aids effectively.

If the horse suspects that he may receive a pull in the mouth from an insecure rider, he will be less likely to want to jump.

CORRECTION

- Improve the position. (See Chapter 3 – Effects of the Rider's Position).

(d) The rider's fear

A horse will sense the rider's fear through tension in his position, and as a result the horse may lose impulsion. If the horse feels that the rider lacks commitment to the fence, it may sap the horse's confidence and cause him to lose impulsion during the approach.

CORRECTION

Seek lessons from a sympathetic instructor, on horses that are used to giving nervous riders confidence.

Find a level in your jumping that you are happy with, and remain at that level until you wish to progress further.

(e) Over-facing the horse

It is very easy for an ambitious rider to push a horse too quickly, especially a horse that seems keen, talented and confident. Pushing a horse to jump a big, technical track too early in his career may result in him losing the desire to jump. Initially you may feel that the horse backs off on the approach to the fence, and this can quickly deteriorate into the horse refusing, which is harder to deal with.

CORRECTION

- Make progress gradual. Watch your horse for any signs that may suggest he is losing confidence, and be quick to rectify the situation.

(f) The bit is too strong

Over-bitting may be the reason for the horse losing impulsion on the approach to a fence.

CORRECTION

- Take advice on which bit might be more suitable.

- When buying a horse, always ask what bit he uses to jump, but never feel that you have to stick with this bit if it does not suit you. Everyone will ride each horse in a slightly different way and will desire a slightly different feel at the end of the reins.

3 THE HORSE RUNS OUT OR REFUSES

Both of these traits are undesirable in a jumping horse, and unfortunately they can become habit-forming in a very short space of time. There are a host of reasons why the horse either runs out or refuses. Often horses who will jump willingly at home realise that when jumping under BSJA rules, two refusals earns elimination, leading them to understand that they do not have to jump any further. They really are that clever!

Although both refusals and run-outs are equally frustrating, run-outs are almost always due to rider error, and show that the rider did not have the horse channelled between leg and hand. If the horse is channelled, he is more likely to either jump the fence or stop.

REASONS FOR REFUSALS/RUN-OUTS

(a) Lack of confidence in horse or rider.

(b) Poor quality canter.

(c) Poor approach.

(d) Rider's positional influence over the horse.

(e) New to competing.

(f) Horse finds distances in competition difficult.

(g) The level jumped is higher/more technical than the horse and rider are used to.

(h) Horse's temperament.

(i) The horse is stale/bored with jumping.

(a) Lack of confidence in horse or rider

See explanation earlier in this chapter.

(b) Poor quality canter

The rider should produce a good quality canter during the warm-up in order for the horse to produce his best jumping efforts. If the canter is not of a good quality, the horse's task is harder.

CORRECTIONS

- Improve the quality of canter through flatwork. See Chapter 2 – Flatwork for Jumping.

LEFT: A refusal.

BELOW: A run-out while approaching a fence on an angle. An angled fence offers the horse a greater opportunity to run out. Keep the horse straight, between hand and leg at all times.

(c) Poor approach

Loss of balance and rhythm during the approach to a fence will result in the horse losing the quality of canter. This could easily lead to a refusal. Approaching the fence at an angle may cause the horse to lose focus on the jump. At the least, it offers him a route to run out of at the side of the fence.

CORRECTIONS

- Work to improve turns by using ground poles initially, instead of fences. By improving the turn, the rider should be able to approach the fence at right angles, on a straight line and maintain the quality of the canter.

(d) Rider's positional influence over the horse.

See Chapter 3 – Effects of the Rider's Position.

(e) New to competing

You will inevitably find that horses behave differently when they compete at shows, compared to the way they are at home. Learning to manage the horse at competitions is simply another aspect to competing. If you are full of nerves, remember that you will be transmitting your feelings to your horse. The more regularly you compete, the easier it will become for both of you.

CORRECTIONS

- Give inexperienced horses time to become used to travelling to competitions, and start by always entering classes that are well within the horse's comfort zone. If competing is made difficult early on, and the horse realises that in competition he

can stop twice and not have to jump any further, a serious problem may develop.

- If you are eliminated in a competition, return to the warm-up arena and ensure that the horse jumps confidently before you finish. Most classes allow you to jump one fence on your way out. Choose a fence that you and the horse were confident with.

- If there are few entries in the class, many competitions will allow a rider to re-enter the class HC – *hors concours* (non-competitively). You will be required to pay again to re-enter, but you may believe it to be beneficial to the horse to return to the ring to jump. To do this, you must be almost certain that the outcome will be significantly better than the previous round, or the problem may be compounded. Remember, a competition is not the time or place to correct a schooling problem – this must be accomplished at home.

(f) The horse finds distances in competition difficult

The training distances that are used at home for doubles and related distances are often shorter than those found in competition. The reason for this is that we like to keep the horse short and bouncy in the canter, in order for the horse to make a better shape over the fence. Sometimes, in competition, the horse may find the distances long or short, depending on the way in which the horse behaves when he is competing. As a result, he may refuse or run out.

CORRECTIONS

- If distances become an issue in competition, then schooling at home must include work using the distances required. Try to make the changes gradually to give the horse time to adjust. Seek professional advice, as the instructor should be able to advise you as to why the distances are causing an issue. Be aware that not every horse will have the scope to cope with the distances used in competition.

(g) The level jumped is higher/more technical than the horse and rider are used to

A horse will very easily lose confidence if he is asked to jump a course that he finds too big or too technical. Even jumping fillers that he has never seen before may require committed riding.

CORRECTIONS
- If you feel that your horse has lost confidence, work at home to regain his trust, and then compete at a lower level, until you feel that the horse is ready to move on again.

Try to ensure that your schooling at home is at least at the height and technicality of your competitions, if not a little more.

(h) Horse's temperament

The horse's temperament has more bearing on his training than any other single aspect. A brave horse with a big heart will invariably try for a rider. A spooky, nervous horse that lacks confidence will require far more time to develop, no matter how talented.

CORRECTIONS
- If you ride a nervous horse, accept that his training will take far longer, as confidence is

incredibly important. You must also develop a feel for when to introduce something new, when to finish a session on a positive note, and when repetition is necessary.

(i) The horse is stale/bored with jumping

With the competitions that are on offer, it is easy to jump all year round. This may suit some horses, but not all. A horse that becomes stale may tell his rider by refusing to jump.

CORRECTIONS
- Within a horse's training programme, try to add variety to keep the horse fresh. You may find that giving the horse a holiday for a week or two is enough to recharge his batteries so that he is banging at the gate, asking to work again!

4 THE HORSE REPEATEDLY JUMPS TO THE LEFT/RIGHT OVER THE FENCE

Maintaining the straightness of the horse when jumping is essential in order to be able to link a series of fences together and allow the horse to make a good shape over the fence.

REASONS FOR JUMPING TO ONE SIDE
(a) Unbalanced canter.

(b) Quality of the canter is different on right/left rein.

(c) Horse has learned to jump to one side.

(d) The rein contact is uneven.

(e) Rider's position affects the horse.

(f) The horse slips on take-off.

(a) Unbalanced canter

See Chapter 2 – Flatwork for Jumping.

(b) Quality of the canter is different on right/left rein

See Chapter 2 – Flatwork for Jumping.

Placing a pole on the side of the fence, on the side towards which the horse is drifting, may aid straightness.

(c) The horse has learned to jump to one side

You may have bought a horse whose previous rider 'taught' it, through the influence of his position, to jump to one side of the fence. This can become a habit, which must be corrected if possible.

CORRECTIONS

- Firstly, check that the canter is even on both reins. Ride around a course of ground poles, keeping the horse between leg and hand on a straight line through the centre of the poles. If the problem is not apparent during the work with ground poles, work over a single cross-pole, aiming to maintain the straightness. Develop a grid of cross poles, again working to keep the straightness. Progress to riding a course of cross-poles.

- If the horse remains straight over cross-poles, but veers to one side when jumping a vertical or spread, place another pole from the edge of the vertical down to the floor on the side that the horse favours. This should encourage him to aim for the centre of the fence.

- Another fence which may be useful is a vertical incorporating a cross-pole. This should help the horse to focus and remain straight over the centre of the fence.

Breaking habits take time. Perseverance is required.

(d) The rein contact is uneven

As the horse stretches his head and neck forwards, the rider should keep a light feel at the end of the reins. If he meets one rein more than the other, this will have the effect of turning him in the air.

This cross-pole and vertical combination helps to maintain straightness.

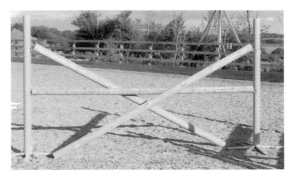

CORRECTIONS

- Ensure that the reins are of an equal length and that your hands soften forwards evenly over the fence.

(e) Rider's position affects the horse

See Chapter 3 – Effects of the Rider's Position.

(f) The horse slips on take-off

This is not uncommon when jumping on grass.

CORRECTION

- Ensure that the horse is using the correct studs for the ground conditions.

5 THE HORSE ALWAYS LANDS ON ONE LEAD LEG

Most horses show favouritism for one lead leg over the other, in the same way that we are right- or left-handed. When jumping a course, if the incorrect lead is not corrected, the horse may become unbalanced on the turns. It is time-consuming to change the lead, and often breaks the rhythm of the

This rider is looking to the left, but tightness in the right rein causes the horse to look to the right, and land on the right canter lead.

canter, so it is far better to ensure that the horse lands on the right lead for the next upcoming turn.

REASONS FOR LANDING ON A SPECIFIC LEAD LEG

- The horse is very one-sided on the flat and this follows through into jumping. See Chapter 2 – Flatwork for Jumping.

- The rider does not try to influence the lead leg. See Chapter 8 – Influencing the Canter Lead.

- The rider is crooked over the fence. See Chapter 3 – Effects of the Rider's Position.

WHENEVER A PROBLEM IS ENCOUNTERED
- Try to understand the issue from the horse's point of view.
- Establish when and why the problem started.
- Seek advice from someone knowledgeable.
- Solve the problem constructively and progressively.

6 POLEWORK

Poles are often only considered valuable as an introduction to jumping for young or green horses. Once the horse has progressed through this stage there are still a great variety of exercises using poles, which will benefit horse and rider.

1 TROT POLES

In addition to being an introduction to jumping for young horses, trot poles are a valuable tool for teaching the horse balance, rhythm and engagement.

trot pole distance
4ft 6ins – 5ft 6ins/1.35m – 1.70m

placing pole distance (trot)
8ft – 9ft/2.45m – 2.75m

TROT POLES AS PREPARATION FOR JUMPING

Basic work begins with one trot pole placed on a straight line, usually the threequarter line, opposite E/B. Develop an understanding for maintaining balance and rhythm through the turn, onto a straight line and to the centre of the pole. Continue this line to the other end of the school.

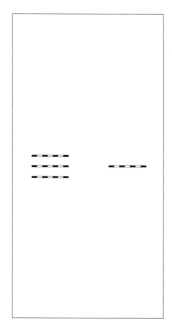

Three trot poles plus a single pole. Start with the single pole on the threequarter line.

During the initial stages, the horse will want to look down at the pole. Allow him to do this, while maintaining the impulsion and keeping him between leg and hand. The horse must be allowed to determine the way in which he should travel over the obstacle. An experienced horse will have the knowledge to traverse ground poles without curiosity.

The next stage is for the horse to trot over more than one pole. Always use an odd number of poles, otherwise the horse has a tendency to jump them in pairs. Place three poles on the opposite side of the school (shown left), and as before, maintain balance and rhythm throughout. Include use of the poles on both sides of the school and on both reins.

Usually at this stage, the second and third poles can be turned into a small cross-pole, leaving the first pole as a placing pole to the jump.

The exercise with three poles can be repeated on the diagonal lines across the school. This is more demanding on the rider, as finding a straight line on the diagonal through the centre of the poles is more difficult than when running parallel to the side of the school.

Again, once the trot pole work is established, the poles can be used to build a small cross-pole.

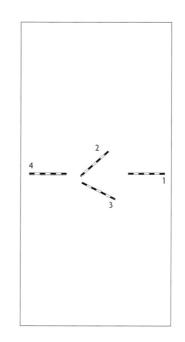

Small course out of trot over poles.

A young horse can begin to develop focus on a course by placing poles randomly around the school and riding a small course out of trot over the poles. There is more information on course riding in Chapter 8.

USING POLES TO HELP A HORSE THAT RUSHES

A horse that rushes to a fence out of trot can be helped by the use of ground poles. Place three trot poles in front of the first fence to help to maintain the horse's balance and rhythm during the approach. The third trot pole will also act as the placing pole.

The exercise can be developed easily into a gird from this point by including a second fence one-non-jumping stride after the first. Grids help the horse to be more athletic, and in this instance

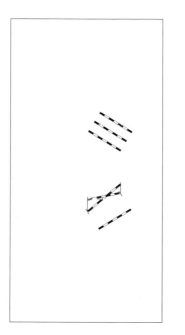

Three trot poles on the diagonal, with a small cross-pole and with a placing pole in front of it.

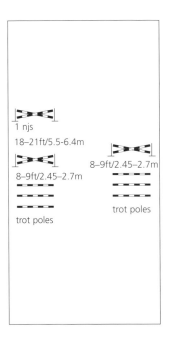

1 njs
18–21ft/5.5-6.4m

8–9ft/2.45–2.7m

8–9ft/2.45–2.7m

trot poles

trot poles

*Using ground poles to help a horse that rushes.
See text.*

should develop the balance and rhythm from the trot into the canter. (See Chapter 7 – Grids and Related Distances.) On departure, encourage the horse to maintain balance and rhythm in the canter for a few strides before returning to trot. This develops the horse's ability to maintain the canter after the fence, which will be required when fences are linked together as a course.

TROT POLES TO IMPROVE ENGAGEMENT

An experienced and reasonably fit horse can develop greater engagement through the use of raised trot poles. As a horse requires engagement in order to propel himself up and over a fence, this is a very valuable exercise. It also adds variety to the work.

Set up three, five, seven or nine trot poles at the correct distance on the threequarter line. The number of poles used depends on the experience and fitness of the horse.

Once the rhythm and balance is established over the poles on the ground, raise alternate ends of the poles, starting with the middle two poles. Raise no more than 20cm (8ins) initially.

Working from the centre towards the outside, gradually raise two more poles each time, until the entire line is raised alternately.

As the horse becomes more confident and stronger, the pole can be raised on both sides, producing an obstacle similar to a cavaletti. Start with the two central poles raised at both ends, while the others are raised alternately on one side only. Eventually, the entire line can be raised on both sides.

*Trot poles with wings
positioned alternately.*

The two central poles raised at one end, alternately.

Four central poles raised alternately.

All poles raised alternately.

Horse trotting over the raised trot poles. Notice the flexion of the knee and hock.

NOTE: This exercise is physically very demanding on the horse. It may take many months to reach the final stage.

2 CANTER POLES

Canter is the most important pace for the jumping horse. Every effort should be put into developing the horse's canter to fulfil his potential. This will take years, as the horse will become stronger and more capable with time. Canter poles can help to teach the horse to develop balance, rhythm and athleticism. They can help the rider to develop a feel for the rhythm of the stride to the fence.

canter pole distance
9ft – 12ft/2.75m – 3.65m

CANTER POLES ON A CIRCLE

Place two or four poles on a 20m circle, evenly spaced apart. Aim to ride the same number of strides in each half or quarter of the circle.

The stride can then be lengthened or shortened, again aiming to have the same number of strides in each part of the circle.

Many riders focus on the poles in this exercise and forget about the shape of the circle. The circle will help you to maintain rhythm and balance in the canter and should therefore be the priority for the exercise to succeed.

CANTER POLES ON A STRAIGHT LINE

Place one pole on one threequarter line, and three canter poles on the other threequarter line.

Practise firstly using the single pole. Focus on maintaining the balance and rhythm of the horse throughout the turn, straight line over the pole and the

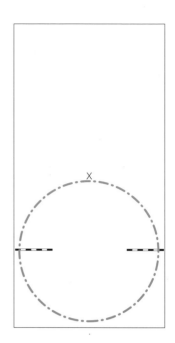

Canter poles on a circle.

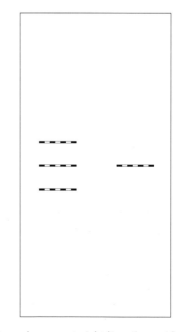

Canter poles on a straight line. Start with a single canter pole on the threequarter line.

turn at the other end of the school.

Once this can be achieved over a single pole, develop the exercise to include the three poles on the opposite side of the school. Work on both reins.

Often when this exercise is ridden, the rider tenses, worrying about meeting the poles correctly. Relax, keep the horse between leg and hand and, to a certain extent, let the horse work it out for himself. The rider is there to support the horse and maintain the rhythm – let the poles teach the horse.

MAINTAINING RHYTHM TO AND FROM A FENCE

The previous exercise can develop directly into this one.

A horse that tends to rush on the approach to or departure from a fence can be helped by using poles to regulate the rhythm of the canter. This exercise addresses both of these faults.

Place a cross-pole at the beginning of what will become a line of canter poles to another fence. If you have any doubt in your ability to place the horse at a good take-off point to the first fence, approach out of trot, using a placing pole in front of the first fence.

Once the cross-pole has been jumped, gradually include the canter poles, one at a time. Use three canter poles the first time the exercise is ridden, increasing up to five poles over time.

Place another cross-pole at the end of the line of poles, where the fourth canter pole would have been positioned. (See diagram overleaf.)

Cross-pole and placing pole.

The main aim of the exercise is to develop balance and rhythm in the canter. Once this is achieved using the cross-poles, the second fence could be built as a vertical or spread, which will further help the horse and rider to develop the confidence to jump these fences out of a rhythm. As the distance between the poles is dependent on the horse's stride, the author recommends that this exercise is ridden under the supervision of a qualified instructor.

This exercise should teach the horse and rider to maintain the rhythm on both the approach to and departure from the fence. The eventual goal is to remove the canter poles, and for the horse and rider to maintain the rhythm and length of stride. The exercise also teaches the horse, and especially the rider, the feel for the stride in a related distance.

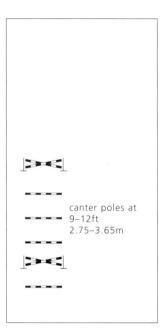

Cross-poles and canter poles set up to help maintain rhythm to and from a fence. (See text on previous page.)

SHORTENING AND LENGTHENING THE STRIDE

Once the horse and rider are able to maintain balance and rhythm in the canter, and are able to keep it throughout the previous exercise, attention can be turned to being able to vary the length of stride in the canter. Poles can help with this as they can be used to create a definite distance for the rider to work with.

Varying the length of stride must firstly be introduced within flatwork exercises. See Chapter 2 – Flatwork for Jumping.

Place two poles on the threequarter line at a training distance suitable for five non-jumping strides (see Appendix) between them.

Practise shortening and lengthening the canter to enable the horse to fit five, six, seven and even eight strides in between the poles, while still maintaining the rhythm of the canter. The number of strides achieved will depend on the horse's level of training and the quality of the canter.

The chosen canter must be established before reaching the first pole, rather than trying to change it once you are in the related distance.

Make the change in the canter progressive, i.e., try not to ride for five strides and then shorten to eight.

For the rider of one horse, this allows you to further develop the feel and ability to vary the length of stride, which should help to create a more harmonious picture during a course. For a rider of many horses, this exercise will allow you to develop

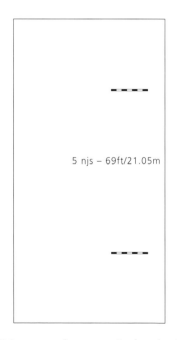

Using two poles to practise lengthening and shortening the canter stride.

a feel for the canter necessary in each horse to achieve the same results.

RAISED CANTER POLES

For exercises using raised canter poles, refer to the exercise 'RAISED TROT POLES' and substitute the distances for trot with the distances for canter poles. The table of distances is found in the Appendix.

Using ground poles, improvement should be seen with any horse that lacks rhythm and balance. Developing the horse's quality of canter is an intrinsic step to developing the horse's jumping ability.

7 GRIDS AND RELATED DISTANCES

Grids are probably the most useful tool for making improvements in jumping, whether the focus is the horse or the rider. The horse can be helped to improve its technique, rhythm, balance, straightness, suppleness, athleticism and confidence. The rider can be helped regarding position, feel for a stride, ability to maintain a rhythm, and confidence.

As a strong, cautionary note, a grid built with distances that do not suit the horse can be counter-productive and, as a result, both horse and rider could greatly lose confidence. If you lack experience in building grids, book lessons and allow your instructor to develop the required grid work safely. Seek professional advice.

Distances in grids depend upon many criteria:

- Size of horse or pony.

- Scope of the horse or pony.

- The reason for training over a grid, for example:

  - developing the rider's position

  - improving the horse's technique

  - teaching the horse to shorten/lengthen the stride between fences

- The surface to be jumped upon.

- The gradient of the ground.

A qualified instructor should be able to take these criteria into consideration to produce a grid that will benefit horse and rider.

If you have experience in building and riding grids, the following exercises show a variety of formats for grids.

For all distances, see the Appendix.

ADVICE FOR GRIDS

- Approaching any grid out of trot tends to produce the best results, unless you are at the stage in your riding when you can virtually guarantee positioning the horse at the initial fence at a good point for take-off. A trot approach will generally require a shorter distance after the fence than will a canter approach.

- Using a placing pole before the first element of the grid will aid the horse to reach the desired point of take-off.

- It is advisable to use a cross-pole as the first fence, as this is not only an inviting fence, but it also helps to encourage the horse and rider to aim for the middle of the grid.

- The natural progression of fences when jumping, should be cross-pole – vertical – spread. This does not mean that the grid sequence needs to be in this order. For example, cross-pole – spread – vertical is a useful exercise for encouraging engagement, but the spread fence should be introduced as a vertical before developing it into a spread.

- The grid must be built progressively, starting with a placing pole to a cross-pole. Add each new element once horse and rider are confident. Although the aim may be to include fences to improve the horse's technique, initially the fences can be introduced as cross-poles and another day, developed into the desired fences. It can be very taxing, both mentally and physically, for a horse that has jumped only single fences to be asked to negotiate two or three fences in a row. Keep new exercises well within the horse's comfort zone initially.

- The types of fence chosen as each element of the grid will be governed by your purpose for using the grid. If, for example, you are working with a horse whose jump is very flat, you might select a cross-pole–vertical–vertical, with one stride in between each element. If your horse needs to learn to stretch over spreads, you might choose cross-pole–ascending spread–ascending spread, with two strides in between each element.

- If you use a spread fence as any element of the grid except the last element, you will need to allow slightly more distance for the canter strides after the spread. This is because the spread, in lengthening the jump, results in the following canter generally being longer also.

BASIC GRIDS ON THE THREEQUARTER LINE, OFF THE RIGHT OR LEFT REIN

CONSIDERATIONS FOR ALL GRIDS

- Approach – rhythm and impulsion of the trot, balance through the turn, straightness of the line, aiming for the centre of the grid.

- Position – do you approach in balanced position or rising trot? This depends on personal preference. Try both methods, and assess which suits you and your horse the best.

- Maintain rhythm throughout the grid.

- Position of the rider – maintain balanced position once in the grid. Do not push with your seat, as you are likely to flatten the canter and therefore the shape of the horse over the jumps. Use your legs to generate energy.

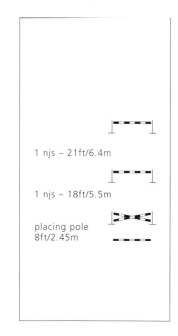

1 njs – 21ft/6.4m

1 njs – 18ft/5.5m

placing pole
8ft/2.45m

Example grid.

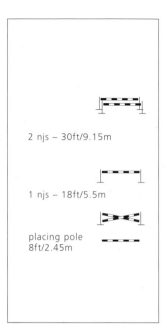

2 njs – 30ft/9.15m

1 njs – 18ft/5.5m

placing pole
8ft/2.45m

Example grid.

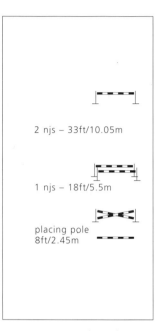

2 njs – 33ft/10.05m

1 njs – 18ft/5.5m

placing pole
8ft/2.45m

Example grid.

• Departure from the grid – rhythm, straight line, balanced turn.

IMPROVING RHYTHM IN A GRID

Canter poles can be used within a grid to encourage the horse to maintain his rhythm. This particularly helps a horse that is prone to rushing.

Develop the grid progressively, adding the preceding jump or canter pole on from the last, each time, assuming the horse is confident and that the jump does not need to be repeated.

Position ground poles in the grid as in the diagram. Again, when riding through, keep the horse balanced between leg and hand, and let the poles help the horse to maintain his rhythm.

Placing poles on the ground after a fence has the

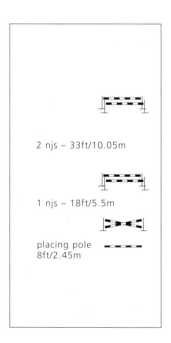

2 njs – 33ft/10.05m

1 njs – 18ft/5.5m

placing pole
8ft/2.45m

Example grid.

added advantage of helping a horse that tends to jump in a hollow or inverted fashion, as it encourages the horse to look down as he jumps the fence, and therefore to work over his back.

INTRODUCING A BOUNCE

A bounce consists of two fences, related to each other without a canter stride in between. The horse lands from the first jump, and immediately takes off to jump the second fence.

Bounces are extremely useful in developing the athleticism and agility of the horse, but are also physically demanding. They can also be mentally demanding when first introduced, as the horse has very little time to determine what he needs to do. It is important that bounces are introduced correctly to develop the confidence required to negotiate them

- Jump the first cross-pole of the grid out of trot using a placing pole in front.

- Place a ground pole in the position where the second element of the bounce will be. Ride through the grid.

- Build the second element of the bounce as a cross-pole also. Ride through the grid. Generally, using cross-poles is sufficient to improve the horse's athleticism, but you could build the second element of the bounce as a vertical if required.

- Add in the last element of the grid, a vertical for a distance of one non-jumping stride

- Throughout, commit the horse to the grid and ride him positively between leg and hand.

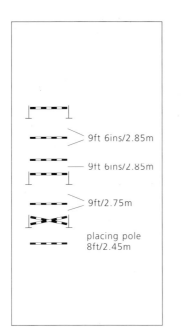

Exercise for improving rhythm in a grid.

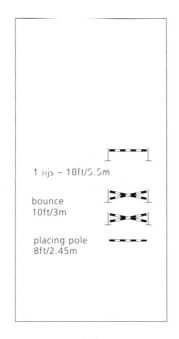

Example bounce.

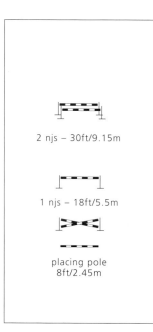

Example centre-line grid.

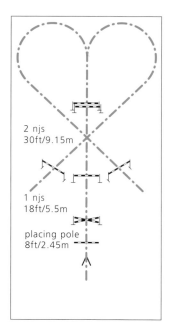

The centre-line grid exercise can be developed to include fences ridden on the diagonal.

GRIDS ON THE CENTRE LINE

Building grids on the centre line offers greater versatility to the exercise, but with this versatility, comes complexity.

- These exercises can be ridden off either rein. However, a turn onto the centre line is more difficult than a turn onto the threequarter line.

- Over the last fence, the rider has the option to influence the canter lead on landing, depending on which way he wishes to turn after the grid. See Chapter 8 – Influencing the Canter Lead. However, the rider must be knowledgeable enough to be able quickly to recognise which lead leg the horse is on, in order to turn in the correct direction.

- The exercise can be developed to include fences to be ridden on the diagonal following the grid.

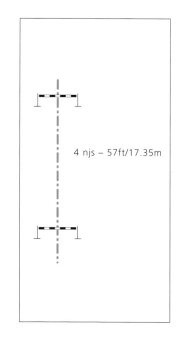

Related distance, in a straight line.

RELATED DISTANCES

A related distance refers to two jumps that are related to each other by between three and five non-jumping strides. These fences may be on a straight line from the first to the second, or set at an angle to each other, known as a 'dog leg'.

AIMS WHEN RIDING A RELATED DISTANCE

- Approach in and maintain a balanced, rhythmical canter.

- Ride a balanced and accurate turn onto the correct line into the fence.

- The strides in the related distance should be of even length, maintaining the rhythm of the canter. Through training, the rider will develop a feel for the horse's length of stride and achieving even strides in a related distance.

- Ride straight away from the fence, maintaining balance and rhythm through the next turn.

Depending on your horse, and the jump over the first element, it is possible, and may be necessary, to alter the set number of strides in a related distance.

Practise, by starting to work with poles, using distances for three, four or five non-jumping strides. (See the Appendix for table of distances.) As with the shortening and lengthening in canter exercise in Chapter 6 – Polework, ride the horse's natural canter over the poles, and aim to achieve the correct number of strides, of even length. Then start to shorten the stride, so that you are able to ride four or five strides in a four-stride distance, and five, six or seven strides in a five-stride distance.

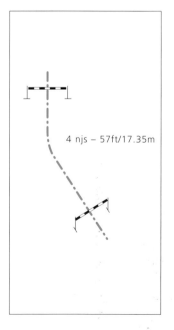

Related distance, on a 'dog-leg'.

4 njs – 57ft/17.35m

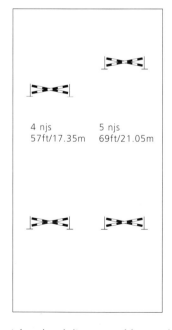

Straight related distances of four and five non-jumping strides.

4 njs
57ft/17.35m

5 njs
69ft/21.05m

Once this is achieved, build cross-poles where the ground poles are. Ride the same exercise as above.

Then build the fences to include verticals and spreads. It is easier, and far safer at this stage to build vertical–vertical, or spread–vertical, than vertical–spread. The reason for this is that if you get the striding wrong to the second element, the horse has only to navigate out of the related distance over a vertical, and does not have to achieve the width of a spread fence.

Begin to feel whether your jump over the first element rode as you expected, or whether you landed short and lost a little impulsion, or even landed long and running. This will determine how you need to ride to the second element.

THREE-STRIDE RELATED DISTANCE

Landed perfectly – maintain rhythm and length of stride. Aim for three strides.

Horse and rider are focused on the second jump. The rider maintains position and the horse maintains rhythm. The rider should be looking up and ahead over the second fence, but the fact that she is not does indicate that she is thinking about the canter lead early.

Landed short – kick on. Keep the horse between leg and hand, and aim for three strides.

Landed long – shorten and aim for three strides.

A distance of three strides does not have room for alteration, unless you have a very short-striding horse. Whatever the jump over the first element, aim for three strides.

FOUR-STRIDE RELATED DISTANCE

Landed perfectly – maintain rhythm and length of stride. Aim for four strides.

Landed short – ride on for four strides, or shorten for five strides. This will depend on the horse, size of fence, ground and gradient of the ground.

Landed long – shorten and aim for four.

FIVE-STRIDE RELATED DISTANCE

Landed perfectly – maintain rhythm and aim for five strides.

Landed short – ride on for five strides, or shorten for six strides. This will depend on the horse, size of fence, ground and gradient of the ground.

Landed long – shorten and aim for five.

As there are so many variables, only through practice will you learn how to adapt instinctively to each situation.

Start now to include related distances across the diagonal, as the turn into and out of the jumps may highlight other issues, such as straightness out of the turn, which will need addressing. This is a valuable exercise, as indoor jumping in the winter season often dictates a shorter approach than does outdoor jumping in the summer.

INTRODUCING 'DOG LEGS'

When walking or building a related distance on a 'dog leg', walk the line on which the fences have been or are to be built. Imagine a line drawn through each fence, at 90° to the centre of these fences. Where the two lines meet is the point at which you turn to the second part of the related distance. The turn should not be sharp, but rounded.

The need to focus the horse on the fence that you wish to jump may sound obvious, but an inability to do so is often the downfall of riders in their early stages of competition. Practising an exercise such as the one below will not only work on related distances, but also communication between horse and rider.

Riding from fence 1 to fence 3 is far harder than riding from fence 3 to fence 1. When riding from 3–1, the first fence that will come into the horse's view after fence 3 will be fence 1. When riding from fence 1–3, the horse will focus initially on fence 2.

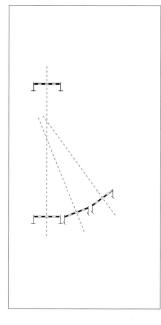

Straight and 'dog leg' related distances, illustrating various lines to be taken.

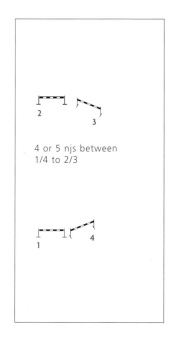

4 or 5 njs between 1/4 to 2/3

Straight and 'dog leg' related-distance exercise.

The rider will need to communicate to the horse that he must jump fence 3.

As you practise this exercise, think not only about the regularity of the strides in the related distance, but also about communication, 'feel' and the partnership that is developing between you and your horse.

Riding accurately through related distances is a huge step towards being ready to ride courses.

8 INFLUENCING THE CANTER LEAD

In order for the horse to maintain balance and rhythm throughout a course, he should be on the correct lead leg around every turn.

Ideally the horse is asked to land on the correct lead leg after each fence so that the rider has one less detail to consider on the approach to the next fence. Unless your horse has been taught to carry out flying changes, it can be a time-consuming process to return to trot and make another transition to canter. Not only will this lose you valuable seconds in a jump-off, but it may also spoil the natural flow and rhythm of the course.

1 THE SEQUENCE OF FOOTFALLS IN THE CANTER

LEFT LEAD CANTER

- Right hind leg
- Left hind leg and right foreleg (as a diagonal pair)
- Left foreleg (known as the 'leading leg')

RIGHT LEAD CANTER

- Left hind leg
- Right hind leg and left foreleg (as a diagonal pair)
- Right foreleg (known as the 'leading leg')

2 RECOGNISING THE LEADING LEG

Initially, you may need to glance down to recognise which canter lead the horse is on, but gradually you should begin to feel it through your seat and legs, and the way that the horse is moving.

When in canter, try firstly to feel whether the horse is balanced or unbalanced as he canters around corners or on a circle. If he feels balanced, he is more than likely on the correct lead leg for the direction in which he is going. If he feels unbalanced, he is probably on the incorrect lead canter.

To check your answer, look down at the horse's front legs. You will see that one foreleg takes the stride further forward than the other. This is the leading leg. So if your horse's left foreleg strides the furthest forward, you are on the left lead canter, which is correct if you are cantering around a left turn.

3 INFLUENCING THE CANTER LEAD OVER THE FENCE

EXERCISE 1

Position a fence where you are able to approach it from a 20m circle off both reins. If you have the use

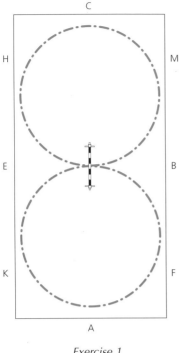

Exercise 1

Approaching out of a balanced, rhythmical and active trot, give the horse the aid for canter for the lead leg that you want, as the horse takes off.

Aids to influence the leading leg:

- **Look in the direction in which you wish to go,** keeping the upper body straight.
- Keeping the **inside leg in position**, draw the **outside leg slightly further back**, without losing the security of the leg. Give the horse the aid for canter with both legs.
- At the same time as using your legs, **maintain the contact on the outside rein, and open the inside rein slightly.** The inside rein should not be used so strongly that you turn the horse, but just enough to allow a little inside flexion, and to indicate the direction in which you will be moving.

Rider's canter aids are variable. Give YOUR canter aid as the horse takes off – you might use more pressure with the outside or the inside leg. Do not change your canter aid as you start to teach the horse a new skill.

of a school, this would be on the centre line at X.

Introduce the exercise by placing a ground pole in between the wings.

Trot a figure-of-eight by riding 2 x 20m circles, which join at X over the pole.

Replace the ground pole with a cross-pole. You will approach the fence out of trot initially, so use a placing pole if you wish before the fence. The fence should be relatively small, but large enough that the horse will jump it, rather than trot over it.

To start off with, select the rein on which the horse is most balanced in the canter. You will be remaining on this rein for the next few circles, until you develop a feel for the aids, and the horse understands what is being asked of him.

Once the exercise is progressing well on one rein, try the opposite rein by working on the other circle. As a word of caution, if the horse has been working on one rein for a time, do not try to change the rein over the fence. Horses are, after all, creatures of habit, and you might just part company if you suddenly wish to turn left, when the horse has just worked on twenty circles to the right!

Removing the placing pole, now repeat the exercise on both reins in the canter.

Once horse and rider are established at this stage, start to ride a continuous figure-of-eight. This will require you to make a change of lead over the fence.

The last stage then is to mix up the exercise between circling on the same rein, and changing the rein on the figure-of-eight. If you make sure that you are consistent with your aids and give the horse adequate time to respond, you should find that not only does the horse maintain a rhythm through the exercise, but also he gives you the feeling that he is waiting for your aids.

The horse approaches in right canter lead, and lands in left canter. Notice that as the horse jumps the fence, the left foreleg has come through to change the lead. This illustrates the necessity for the rider to give the aid during take-off in order for the horse to respond.

EXERCISE 2

This is the same as the previous exercise, but ridden on a three-loop serpentine.

The horse will require more balance and co-ordination than for the previous exercise, as the turns are sharper. The rider will need to be able to think ahead and react more quickly, in order to maintain the horse's balance and rhythm.

This is also a great exercise for developing the thought preparation, control, balance and co-ordination required to ride successful turns in a jump-off.

EXERCISE 3

To develop the exercise further, position one fence on both diagonal lines.

Again, riding a figure-of-eight, ask for a change of canter lead over each fence.

This exercise is harder than the previous two

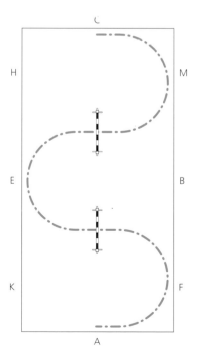

Exercise 2

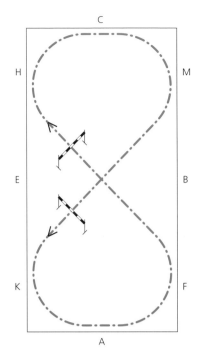

Exercise 3

exercises, as the line through the fence is straight. The curve of the circle in exercise 1 helped the horse to choose the correct lead. This exercise is far closer to the sort of lines found in competition, and therefore needs to be mastered before riding a course. It requires far more rider influence over the horse.

If, when riding this exercise, the horse falls in after the fence, you know that you are using too much inside rein when giving the aids for the lead leg. The line of departure must remain straight in order for the horse to maintain balance and rhythm in the canter and be given maximum space for the approach to the next fence.

NOTE: Try to develop your ability to influence the canter lead over a fence before embarking on riding a course. This aid, which will become automatic, will make learning to ride a course much more simple.

9 COURSES

There are many reasons why horses and riders learn to jump. These include:

- enjoyment
- improving the horse's athletic ability
- conquering a fear
- adding variety within a training programme
- competitive riding

For most riders, jumping a course successfully is the main goal, as the ability to ride a course is the result of many hours of dedicated training. Success must not only be judged on attaining a clear round (although that is obviously most satisfying!), but also on the quality of the round.

When putting a course together, the fences do not have to be large, and could initially consist of just three cross-poles. This would give you the opportunity to analyse where more work is needed before progressing. Equally, if you wish to ride competitively, you must practise riding a course of eight to ten fences before embarking on competitions. Practice is also needed for riding in jump-offs.

In the UK, the governing body for the sport, the British Show Jumping Association (BSJA), has different levels of classes. At the lower levels, course designers build the courses to flow easily. At this early stage they do not want to catch out any horses and riders, so courses are not technically difficult.

As the classes become more advanced, the fences not only become larger, but also the courses increase in technical difficulty, testing ability and the communication between horse and rider.

For Table of Distances, see the Appendix.

1 USING GROUND POLES TO CREATE A COURSE

Often, when riders are faced with a course of fences, all that they see in the early stages are the jumps; thoughts about the important parts in between the jumps are forgotten. By riding a course over poles, the rider can focus on the thought process required in order to produce a flowing round. Once the rider's reactions become automatic over the poles, and the course flows, maintaining rhythm, balance, impulsion and straightness, this is the time that fences can be introduced.

Thought-process when riding a course

Try to look at the course as a whole, rather than individual fences. Each course has a pattern, a route. You must ride that route and commit the horse to jumping the fences within it, aiming to maintain rhythm and balance throughout.

- Set the horse up in a balanced and rhythmical

Horse and rider are focused on the next fence.

canter to the best of your ability and his.

- Look for your first pole.

- Visualise the line through the pole that you must turn onto.

- Maintain the canter through the turn.

- As you ride towards the first pole, be aware of where the next pole is.

- Maintain the straightness of your line on departure.

- Rebalance the canter and change the canter lead if necessary. Regain the rhythm after the change of lead leg.

- Maintain the rhythm through the turn after the first pole, looking for the line into your next pole.

- On reaching the last pole, try to imagine that there is another one afterwards, and ride positively on departure before returning to walk. It is no

secret that many riders have the last fence down because they lack the focus into the last and relax too early. Breathe a sigh of relief on exiting the arena, not before the last fence!

2 BUILDING SHORT COURSES

When warming up to ride a course, jump several practice fences. If you are planning to include cross-poles, verticals and spreads in the course, then these types of fence must have been jumped, usually in that order, as warm-up fences. Warm up over the same height as you will be jumping in the course.

Using the exercises above, replace the ground poles with fences. Build fences that are well within your own and the horse's comfort zone, so that you can concentrate on maintaining the balance, rhythm, impulsion and straightness of the horse in canter around the course.

Try to focus on riding the whole course, and not let your mind think only about the fences.

When training at home, use each round as a schooling round. This means that if you lose balance and rhythm during the course, rather than losing the quality and keeping going, circle before the next fence in order to regain the rhythm, and then continue. In this way, horse and rider learn to maintain the quality of the canter. Gradually, you will feel the loss more quickly, and be able either to prevent it from happening, or have the quickness of reactions to regain it more quickly, and not need to circle. Be careful that you do not become reliant on circling, as in competition this would incur four faults. It is simply a method of schooling to help the horse and rider when necessary.

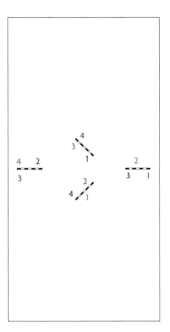

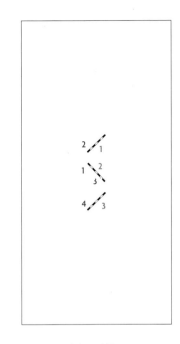

Three permutations of the same course.

Two permutations of the same course.

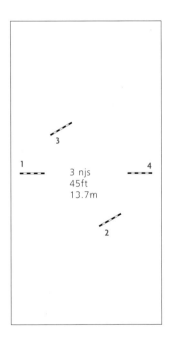

3 njs
45ft
13.7m

Course including a related distance.

3 TURNING SHORT COURSES INTO LONGER COURSES

By building the fences in the previous exercises so that they can be jumped from both directions, a course of eight fences can be designed from four. The fences have to be built so that they are identical from both sides and have ground lines for both directions. Ascending spreads cannot be jumped from both directions. If a spread is to be used, it needs to be a parallel.

As the rider becomes more used to riding courses and the confidence of horse and rider develops, the fences can gradually be built to the height that you are aiming towards. Fillers can also be introduced. (See Chapter 4, Fences to Improve the Horse's Technique, which explains how to introduce the horse to fillers and build fences with correct ground lines.)

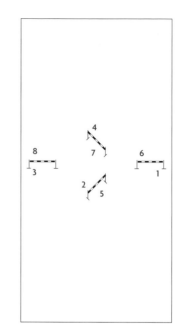

Eight jumping efforts from four fences.

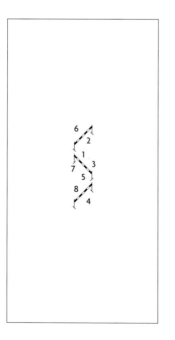

Eight jumping efforts from three fences.

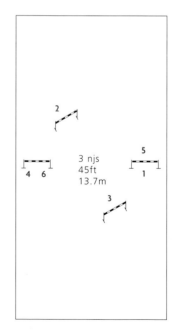

A six-jump course from four fences.

4 BUILDING AND RIDING A COURSE IN PREPARATION FOR COMPETITION

When building a course in preparation for competition, try to include:

- fillers

- a double – one or two strides

- two related distances

CONSIDERATIONS IN COURSE DESIGN

- The first fence should be inviting, such as an ascending spread. Though inviting, it will need positive riding, which is exactly what you need to establish the canter for the course.

- The double should come in the middle of the course. This allows horse and rider time to gain confidence and settle into a rhythm in order to be able to jump the double confidently.

- The double usually consists of a spread and a vertical. Build the spread as the first element, the vertical the second. This means that if the jump into the double is not good, the horse only has to jump out over a vertical, rather than making the width of a spread.

- Placing the more tricky fences, such as the double and spooky fillers, against the side of the school helps to prevent run-outs.

- Try to build the fences without any sharp turns on the approach.

- If jumping outside, think about the gradient of the land. Try to build the more difficult fences, such as

the double or a related distance, on the flat, or slightly up a hill.

RIDING ON UNDULATING GROUND

When riding **uphill**, keep the horse between leg and hand to **maintain the impulsion and length of stride**.

When riding **downhill**, maintain the rhythm, but try to **shorten the stride to keep the horse's hind legs underneath him**. The gradient will result in a landing further away from the fence than normal, and therefore, the shorter stride will help you to reach the next fence correctly.

At this stage you should not need to ride too many circles in between the fences to maintain rhythm. Treat the exercise as a schooling round, and circle only if necessary.

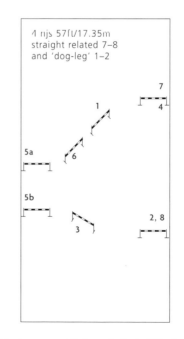

4 njs 57ft/17.35m
straight related 7–8
and 'dog-leg' 1–2

Basic course. Little technical difficulty.

5 INCREASING THE TECHNICALITY OF THE COURSE

Before thinking about making the fences bigger, increase the technicality of the course. Simply moving the fences into a different position will change the demands made on horse and rider.

Making a course more technical

- Position the double on the diagonal.

- Approach the related distance so that there are two possible fences for the horse to see in front of him – one directly in front, one on a dog-leg. Riding to the dog-leg will be harder as the horse will be focused on the fence directly in front.

- If jumping outside, have the approach to a vertical or planks on a slight downhill gradient. The rider must keep the canter engaged.

- Position a related distance slightly downhill: spread – vertical on four or five strides. The rider must keep the canter engaged. This exercise is difficult, as the spread and the gradient will encourage the horse to lengthen and flatten the stride.

6 PRACTISING JUMP-OFF TURNS

Many riders believe that riding in a jump-off is purely about speed. Speed generally creates a long, flat canter and this often results in the horse taking fences down, because the jump is flat.

Teaching the horse to ride tight turns to the fences in a slightly more up-beat canter is likely to be far more successful for the competitive rider. Again, victory will only be achieved from diligent work at home. The horse and rider must learn to ride a jump-off in exactly the same way that the partnership developed during work towards riding a course.

It is of great benefit if the horse is trained to jump fences on an angle, because then the turns ridden can be even tighter. See Chapter 10 – Indoor Cross-Country.

Initial work for jump-offs can be ridden on the flat, simply by using ground poles. Skills learned during the flatwork exercise 'cantering on a square', will

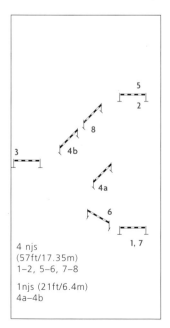

4 njs
(57ft/17.35m)
1–2, 5–6, 7–8

1njs (21ft/6.4m)
4a–4b

A more technical course.

Remember that riding sharp turns can put a lot of stress on the horse's body, especially the legs. Practise jump-off turns in moderation.

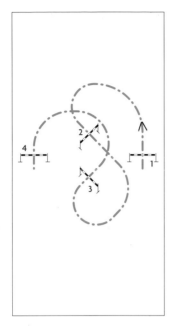

This simple course can be utilised for jump-off practice.

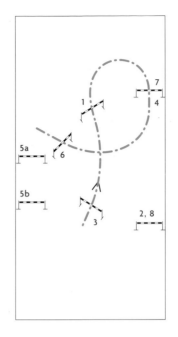

Course 1 jump-off: 3, 1R, 7, 6.

help you to control the horse's shoulders during the turns.

Build the number of fences in the jump-off slowly. Start by linking the first two together, but maintain the same pace in the canter. Once the horse understands what is being asked of him, then the canter can be pushed on a little.

Ride each turn separately before trying to link the four fences together. Experiment by approaching each fence on an angle to see if this helps the turn to the following fence. It may, in fact, make the turn simply too tight. Try turning your horse slightly in the air, as he is jumping the fence. Each horse is different. The rider needs to find what works best with his horse. However you approach the turns, remember that you must communicate well with your horse for him to be able to achieve what you

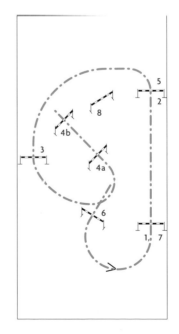

Course 2 jump-off: 6, 7, 2, 3, 4a, 4b.

This long, fast canter made turning difficult. The jumps took 6 seconds to complete. Compare this photo with the one below.

want. You must also learn to think quickly, and ahead of where you are.

Return to the courses that you built in preparation for jumping in competition (pages 77 and 78). Practise jump-offs from these courses, as shown on the previous page.

This short canter enabled a tighter turn, and the fences were jumped in 4.5 seconds. Although the rider's position is less than perfect over the fences, notice the angled approach to the first fence, and how the rider is turning the horse as he jumps.

7 VERSATILE EXERCISES

Here is a selection of exercises that could be set up and left in place for a few days. The exercises are versatile enough that a different aspect of jumping can be worked on each day.

TWO-JUMP EXERCISES

Two jumps are relatively easy to move around, and can be put to good use to train different aspects of jumping.

The next three exercises are useful in working towards maintaining rhythm.

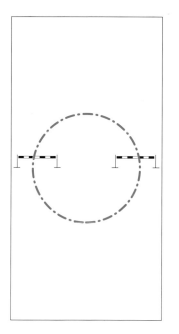

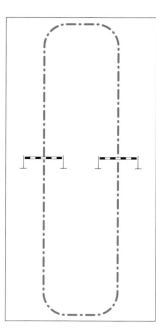

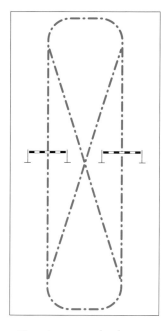

Two jumps on a circle.

Two jumps on the threequarter line.

Changing canter lead across the diagonal

Two jumps on a circle

Jump both fences on a 20m circle. Ask for the correct lead leg every time. You should achieve the same number of strides on each half of the circle. Repeat on the other rein.

Two jumps on the threequarter line

Ride the threequarter line on both sides of the school, jumping the fence on both sides. If the rhythm is maintained, you should meet the fences at roughly the same point of take-off each time. Work to develop consistency. Repeat on both reins.

Changing canter lead across the diagonal

Ride the threequarter line over one fence. Change the rein across the diagonal, changing the canter lead at X through trot or walk. Ride along the other threequarter line and over the fence. Change the rein across the long diagonal, again changing canter lead at X. Work to establish the rhythm immediately after the change of lead.

FOUR-JUMP KITE

This is a highly versatile and challenging exercise. Build the exercise to the distances provided.

Ridden as a related distance

- Ride the related distance up the centre line. Approach firstly out of trot, developing the exercise into canter when horse and rider are ready.

- Focus on maintaining an even length of stride in the related distance, and on holding the rhythm.

- Recognise which canter lead the horse has landed on after the second part of the related distance and turn in the correct direction.

- Give the aids for a specific canter lead over each element. This may be both left, both right, or one left and one right.

Riding the exercise as a short course

- Ride through the related distance. Ask for a specific lead leg on landing after the second fence.

- Turn in the correct direction for the canter lead given.

- Go large and jump the fence on the threequarter line on the opposite side of the school.

- Continue around to the other fence on the threequarter line.

- You are aiming for straight lines and balance and rhythm throughout.

- Repeat on the other rein.

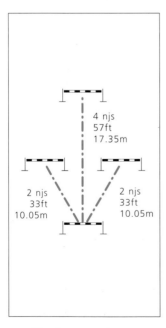

The four-jump kite.

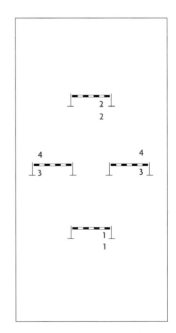

Using the four jumps as a short course.

Jumping the fences on an angle

(Introducing the horse to jumping fences on an angle can be found in Chapter 10 – Indoor Cross-Country.)

• Start to teach the horse to approach a fence on an angle by using the fences on the threequarter line individually.

• Then introduce the fences on the centre line individually.

• Link two fences together, both ridden on the angle, one from the centre line on two non-jumping strides to one on the threequarter line.

• Linking two fences together is always difficult when the horse, up until that point, has only been working with one. Make sure that you focus the horse on the second fence, and keep him between leg and hand to maintain straightness.

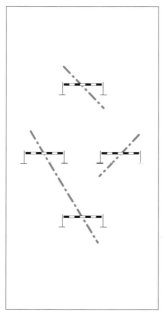

Jumping the four fences on an angle.

Using the exercise to practise jump-off turns

Ride each link from fence to fence individually first, i.e. 1–2, 2–3, 3–4, 4–5.

Ride the five-fence jump-off, remembering the mental notes that you made about each turn.

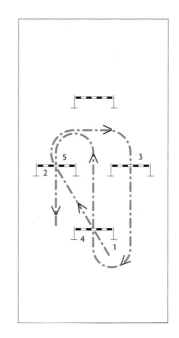

Using the four fences to practise jump-off turns.

8 WALKING THE COURSE AT A COMPETITION

At the entrance to the arena there should be a plan of the course. This will include the jump-off course, which you will also need to walk. Positive thinking and good riding will get you to the jump-off!

Many competitions are ridden as 'two phase'. This term means that if you go clear in the first round, you immediately ride the jump-off. A bell will sound at the end of the first round if you have not been clear, which signals you to not continue to the jump-off.

When walking the course, walk the exact lines that you intend to ride. Walk each distance in a double or a related distance. You then will know whether the distance will ride long, short or just right for your horse, and therefore how you should approach it.

When walking the distances in between fences, walk two human strides (approx. 3ft /90cm each) for landing, four human strides (approx. 12ft/10.8m) for each canter stride, and allow two human strides for the take-off to the next fence.

Example – a 1 non-jumping stride double
This will walk on eight human strides:

2 = landing from first element

4 = one canter stride

2 = take-off for second element

8 human strides

When walking a related distance on a 'dog-leg', walk the line as it has been built, so that you know when you should make the turn. See Chapter 7 – Grids and Related Distances.

Remember that horses are often very different in temperament when out competing from the way they are at home, especially when competing is a novelty. This fact, combined with inevitable rider nerves, often results in the horse having a more forward and ground-covering canter stride than normal. Accept this, and work with it. The distances in competition will be slightly longer than the training distances you use at home, and therefore a slightly bigger canter should work well.

Try to ignore over-heard conversations when walking the course. You do not need other people's fears to add to your own! Riding in with an attitude that one particular fence will cause a problem, just because you over-heard someone say so, is likely to turn your thought into a self-fulfilling prophecy.

Nerves often disappear once you start the course, as riding will take all of your attention. Try to remember any weak areas that you know need most attention, such as turning while maintaining control of the horse's shoulders.

Accept that riding at competition will initially be a steep learning curve, not only regarding riding, but also organising your entries and finding the correct ring! It is the responsibility of every competitor to have read the BSJA Rule Book before entering. Most unaffiliated competitions will be run under the BSJA rules also. The rule book is obtainable from the BSJA directly.

Try always to be positive about your rounds. If problems occur while competing – and they do not occur at home – they may disappear once the novelty and excitement of competing has worn off for you and the horse. Work on the issues at home, and if the problems still occur only in competition, take a qualified instructor with you to a venue that hires out its course, and work on the problems there. Asking a friend to video the rounds will help you to see where further improvements can be made. Most importantly, remember all that you have already achieved to be in a position to compete – and that you are riding for enjoyment!

10 INDOOR CROSS-COUNTRY

Cross-country schooling can be a valuable part of a horse's training, even if eventing is not the end goal. For a horse that is being trained primarily for show jumping, cross-country schooling tends to improve confidence and accuracy, and adds variety to the horse's training schedule.

Training horses to jump fences on an angle will save valuable seconds in a jump-off, and developing the accuracy required to successfully negotiate an arrowhead will aid the approach to any fence.

Whenever introducing a new concept to a horse, always drop the height of the fences down so that

the horse is well within his comfort zone, and finds the exercise easy and fun. This way, horse and rider are not over-faced and have time to focus on what is required.

Simulated fences can be made with comparative ease within a school or field. Even if you are planning to use a local course, it may be wise to carry out some homework over simulated fences initially.

1 JUMPING FENCES ON AN ANGLE

Very often during a cross-country course, horses will be asked to jump fences on an angle. From a show-jumping point of view, this teaches the horse to be confident and honest enough to jump fences on an angle, which will undoubtedly save valuable seconds in a jump-off.

AIM – To ride a straight line through the middle of the three fences, with the distance at one non-jumping stride to one non-jumping stride.

RIDER'S MENTAL PREPARATION – This exercise is far easier than it would appear initially to horse and rider. If the horse is able to jump confidently through a grid of one stride to one-stride verticals, this is a very achievable exercise. The rider must be able to

Jumping three fences at an angle.

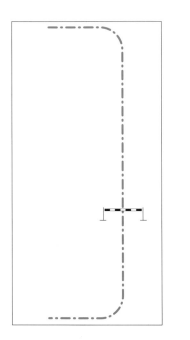

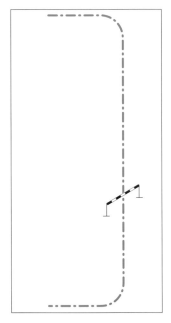

(a) Begin with a straight vertical on the threequarter line.

(b) Start to develop an angle.

(c) Jump the first fence at the desired angle.

see the straight line that runs through the centre of the fences and, from a good approach, hold the horse on that line.

DEVELOPING THE EXERCISE

- Warm up as you would normally. Your warm up should conclude with a vertical at the height that you will be jumping for the rest of the exercise, and the approach should be in canter.

- Although initial thoughts might suggest that cross-poles would be suitable, as they help to guide the horse to the middle of the fence, verticals are easier for the horse to negotiate as they look less confusing within this exercise.

- Place the first vertical in position, at right angles to the line that you are going to jump. Repeat the jump several times, each time angling the fence more than the last until the desired angle is reached. (Not more than 40° to the jumping line.) See diagrams (a)–(c).

- The rider must prioritise the straightness of the line on the approach, the jump and the departure for the exercise to develop successfully.

- Position the second fence on the correct angle, with a distance of one non-jumping stride (21ft/6.4m) between the two fences, measured from the centre of each fence. See diagram (d).

- Approach the fences, maintaining absolute accuracy on the straight line through the centre of the two fences and on departure. Keep the horse channelled straight between leg and hand.

- Once the horse is confident over the two elements, add the third by the same method as the second. Position it again at one non-jumping stride (21ft) away from the second, the distance

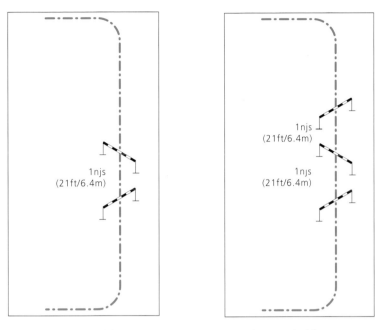

(d) Add the second fence, on
    an angle.

(e) Three angled fences.

being taken from the centre of the fences. See
diagram (e) above.

- Ride through with the same determination to
  maintain the straightness of the line.

- Having ridden three angled fences in a row,
  returning to riding individual fences on angles
  should now seem quite simple. Practise riding
  some of the earlier jump-off exercises and try to
  cut the corners a little more, which will mean
  that you approach each fence on slightly more of
  an angle. Depending on how genuine and
  confident the horse is, and the trust and
  communication between horse and rider, you may
  be surprised at what you and the horse can
  actually achieve.

2 NARROW FENCES

Narrow fences require precise riding. An exercise
that improves the rider's sense of straightness, co-
ordination of the aids and approach to a fence will
undoubtedly improve the rider's ability to control
the horse within a show jumping round. Naturally,
training over narrow fences will also help with
'styles', which are found in some show jumping
courses.

AIM – To ride an accurate line to the middle of
narrow fences, positioned on a mini course in the
school or field.

RIDER'S MENTAL PREPARATION – In truth, we all
aim to approach the centre of the fence. Riding
towards a narrow fence simply leaves less room for
error. Maintain the line that you have chosen by

keeping the horse between leg and hand at all times.

DEVELOPING THE EXERCISE

- Cut poles to approximately 6ft/1.8m in length. Traditionally styles are rustic, but initially painting a band of colour on the centre of the pole will offer the rider a point to aim for. This will also help the rider to identify whether they are jumping over the middle of the pole.

- Warm up as normal, so that you are jumping a vertical of the height that the exercise will be set at. Again, this should be well within the horse and rider's comfort zone.

- Place the shortened pole on the ground between two wings and approach firstly in trot and then canter off both reins, practising the very accurate approach and departure on the straight line through the centre of the pole. Riding this exercise using a ground pole initially also offers the horse time to become used to having a narrower distance between the wings. Some horses can start the exercise by exhibiting caution about the smaller space.

- Once the horse and rider are achieving accuracy and consistency, build a small cross-pole. Once this is jumped confidently, it can be turned into a vertical.

To develop the exercise into a greater challenge

(a) Position the narrow fence on various diagonal lines in the school. The turn onto the diagonal will challenge the rider in a greater way than turning onto the long side of the school as the diagonal line is harder to visualise.

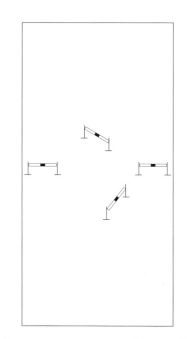

Riding a course over narrow fences will make a normal course feel like child's play.

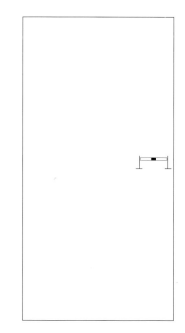

Single narrow vertical developed from a ground pole.

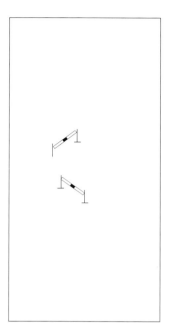

*(a) Narrow fences on the diagonal leave no room
for error during the turns.*

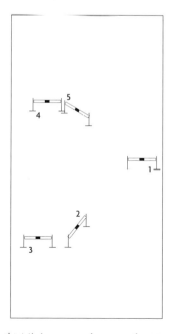

(b) Mini-course of narrow fences.

(b) Design a mini course of narrow fences. This could include a related distance. A related distance on a dog-leg would be an even greater challenge.

Once these exercises have been achieved, return to jumping a course using the traditional length of pole. Not only should this seem easier, but having ridden an exercise that requires a higher level of accuracy, the rider should now be more aware of the level of control that is required to improve the turn and straightness in the approach and departure.

3 ARROWHEADS

Although never found in a show jumping course, training over arrowheads develops directly from jumping narrow fences and will further develop understanding of the control required to be accurate and build the partnership between horse and rider.

AIM – To ride an accurate line over the arrowhead, from both directions.

MENTAL PREPARATION OF THE RIDER – As always, our aim is to maintain balance, rhythm and straightness of the horse by keeping him between leg and hand on the approach and during the departure. This exercise is slightly more demanding than the narrow fences as there are no wings to help to guide the horse to the centre.

DEVELOPING THE EXERCISE
- Warm up as normal. Set up the exercise as shown overleaf, placing the short pole on blocks, rather than wings. The pole to be jumped can be shorter than that used for the narrow fences, as there are no wings on either side (approx. 4ft/1.2m). The

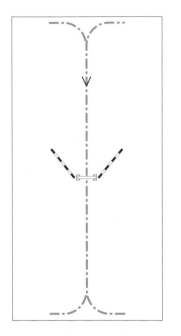

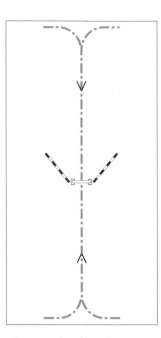

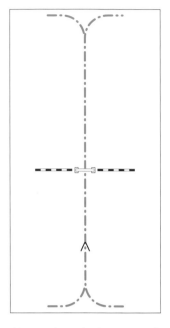

Arrowhead set-up, with short pole on blocks, and angled ground poles.

The arrowhead can be jumped from either direction.

Narrow fence in the centre of two poles

two longer poles, used to create the 'V', should be sufficiently wide apart, so that the horse feels channelled towards the fence, rather than trapped.

• Keeping the horse on a straight line, channelled between leg and hand, ride confidently through the centre of the arrowhead, to jump out over the narrow pole. Keep the leg on at all times, and expect a larger jump than normal, as the horse will probably give this 'new' fence more height than normal. Repeat until the horse feels confident.

• Jumping the arrowhead from the opposite direction requires greater accuracy, as there are no poles to help to guide the horse. Make the exercise progressive, rather than attempting immediately to jump the fence from the opposite direction.

(a) Begin with the fence as a straight line, the narrow pole in the centre. Continue to work at this stage

until you are confident that you are able to meet the centre of the fence every time.

(b) Gradually create the 'V' with the longer poles, allowing the horse and rider time to adjust to the exercise and develop an understanding of the

Jumping out of an arrowhead.

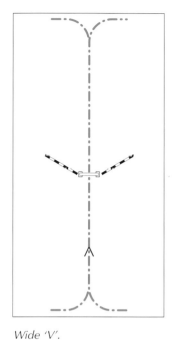

Wide 'V'.

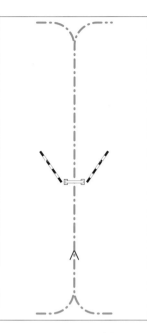

Return to the original fence

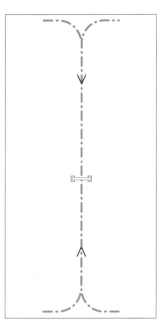

Remove the longer poles for an even greater challenge.

questions being asked.

(c) Having completed the exercise, the horse should be confident to jump the fence from both directions, maintaining rhythm and balance throughout.

(d) A greater challenge now is to remove the longer poles and jump the shortened poles on the blocks. This can also be jumped from both directions.

Jumping into an arrowhead.

Jumping an arrowhead without wings requires great accuracy, communication and trust.

4 CORNERS

Corners are another test of accuracy. They combine approaching a fence on an angle with a narrow fence. Often at the lower levels of eventing, course designers plant a shrub at the point of the corner, which, to a certain extent, acts as a wing. When practising at home, try to use a block at the point of corner, unless you encounter a problem. Training over challenging fences is then going to make the competition seem easier. Remember to keep the size of the fence within the horse's comfort zone during initial training.

AIM – To ride the correct line over a corner.

MENTAL PREPARATION OF THE RIDER – Aim to ride a line at right angles to the line that bisects the corner. Corners often start out as an optical illusion to riders and horses. The line to the fence is important, as the wrong line will result in a greater jumping effort than necessary.

Jumping a parallel which will be developed into a corner.

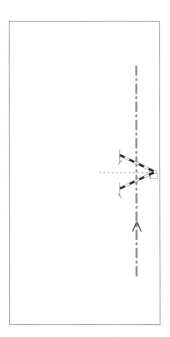

Correct approach line for a corner.

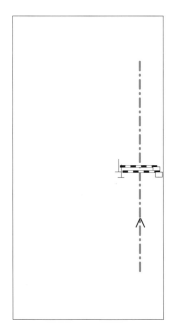

A parallel spread, with blocks at the end where the point of the corner will be.

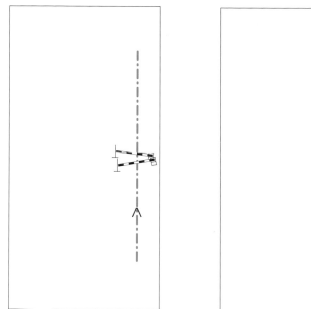

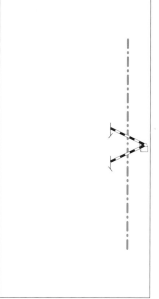

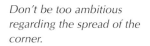

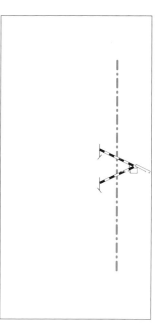

Gradually create the angle of the corner.

Don't be too ambitious regarding the spread of the corner.

Initially, a sloping pole from the point of the corner may help prevent run-outs.

DEVELOPING THE EXERCISE

- Warm up as normal, to include jumping a parallel spread. Use blocks at the end where the point of the corner will be, and blocks or wings at the other end.

- Gradually develop the oxer into a corner by widening one side, and narrowing the other. Do not become too ambitious, and make the corner too wide. It is always better to underestimate the ability of horse and rider. The exercise is designed for accuracy, not as a test of jumping ability. See diagrams above.

- Complete the exercise by successfully jumping a corner that is within the scope of horse and rider.

- If the horse shows any signs of wishing to run out, repeat the earlier stages until they are jumped

In both this photo and the preceding one, the rider needs to have her stirrups shorter to encourage greater security and less extreme movement in her position.

Jumping the corner.

with confidence. If the problem only develops when the fence becomes a corner, school over a small-angled corner, using a wing instead of a block initially. Alternatively, run a pole sideways, out from the point of the corner to the ground. This can be removed once the horse and rider become more disciplined. (See diagram top right. on previous page.)

Improving the versatility of your horse by including cross-country schooling should develop a more trusting, confident, able and co-ordinated partnership.

APPENDIX

TABLE OF DISTANCES

TROT POLES	4ft 6ins – 5ft 6ins	1.35m – 1.70m
CANTER POLES	9ft – 12ft	2.75m – 3.65m
PLACING POLE (TROT)	8ft – 9ft	2.45m – 2.7m

	TRAINING DISTANCE	COMPETITION DISTANCE
BOUNCE	9ft – 11ft/2.75m – 3.35m	11ft – 12ft/3.35m – 3.65m
1 STRIDE	18ft – 21ft/5.50m – 6.40m	24ft/7.30m
2 STRIDES	30ft – 33ft/9.15m – 10.05m	36ft/10.95m
3 STRIDES	45ft/13.70m	48ft/14.65m
4 STRIDES	57ft/17.35m	60ft/18.30
5 STRIDES	69ft/21.05m	72ft/21.95m

The above distances will suit most horses. For ponies, consult the BSJA rule book or discuss with your instructor.

ALSO AVAILABLE

Available from good bookshops and saddlers, or direct from
Kenilworth Press, Wykey House, Wykey, Shrewsbury, SY4 1JA tel: 01939 261616
fax: 01939 261606 or visit the website: **www.kenilworthpress.co.uk** to order on-line